The Staying Sober Workbook

Proprietary Statement

ISBN 978-0-8309-0621-5
Printed in the United States of America

Published by
Herald Publishing House/Independence Press
1001 West Walnut St.
Independence, MO 64050-3562
1-800-767-8181 or 816/521-3015
Fax: 816/521-3066

The Staying Sober Workbook

A Serious Solution for the Problem of Relapse

Based on
The CENAPS® Model of Treatment

Developed by
The CENAPS® Corporation
13194 Spring Hill Drive
Spring Hill, FL 34609
352/596-8000

Terence T. Gorski
President

Herald Publishing House/Independence Press
Independence, Missouri

Table of Contents

Introduction

Most people relapse because they don't understand what relapse is and how to prevent it. With a relapse prevention plan you can identify early warning signs that lead to relapse and learn to manage these warning signs while sober. This workbook is to be used as a supplement to *Staying Sober: A Guide For Relapse Prevention* by Terence T. Gorski and Merlene Miller. *Staying Sober* will help you understand relapse. This workbook will help you develop a plan to prevent it.

Relapse is a process that begins long before people start drinking or drugging. Most people return to alcohol and drug use because they experience a sequence of problems which causes them to become so dysfunctional in sobriety that a return to chemical use seems like a reasonable choice. The pathway into dysfunction includes changes in attitudes, thoughts, feelings, and behaviors. These changes are often referred to as "stinking thinking" or "building up to drink."

You may never use alcohol or other drugs and still be a victim of the relapse process. You can become dysfunctional in sobriety without using alcohol or other drugs. In AA this is called a "dry drunk." These dry drunks should always be taken seriously because they can lead to wet drunks.

You can interrupt the relapse process before you start using alcohol and drugs if you learn to recognize the warning signs that indicate that you are moving away from recovery and toward relapse. This workbook is intended to help you identify your own personal relapse warning signs, learn to recognize them when they occur, and make a plan to interrupt them when you become aware of them.

Relapse prevention planning is for persons who have accepted the fact that they are suffering from an addictive disease and can no longer control the use of alcohol or other drugs. It is intended to complement, *not replace*, other self-help groups and regular alcoholism or drug dependence treatment or counseling. If you are in counseling or therapy, discuss this workbook with your therapist. Self-help groups and professional counseling need to be vital parts of any relapse prevention plan.

When you have finished this workbook you will have a plan to help you progress in recovery and avoid relapse. You may use the workbook alone, with a counselor, or with a group.

Do each exercise thoroughly. Read the directions carefully and answer each question as directed. Each question is important and so is each of your answers. Everything should be done in the order it is presented. Skipping answers or exercises will leave you unprepared for the exercises in the next section of the workbook. Be as thorough and honest in answering the questions as you can. Remember, without rigorous honesty nothing will be gained by doing these exercises.

PART 1

Assessment

1
Stabilization Checklist

Instructions: In order to develop a relapse prevention plan you must first stop using alcohol and drugs and become stable enough in your abstinence to think clearly, manage your feelings and emotions, and remember things. The following questions are designed to help you evaluate if you are currently abstinent and how stable your abstinence is. Answer each question as honestly as you can.

1. Do you believe you are addicted to alcohol or drugs?

   ☐ Yes   ☐ No   ☐ Unsure   (Please explain your answer.)

   _____

   _____

   _____

   _____

   Note: This workbook is designed to be used by people who believe that they are addicted to alcohol and drugs. If you don't believe you are addicted, it would be helpful to set up an appointment with a certified addictions counselor to discuss what addiction is and whether or not you are addicted. You are probably addicted to alcohol and drugs if you are reading this book because you have tried to control your drinking and failed or because you have tried to stay sober and have been unable to do so.

2. Have you stopped using alcohol and drugs?   ☐ Yes   ☐ No

   Note: If you answered *yes,* congratulations! Abstinence is the first step to renewed recovery and relapse prevention. If you answered *no,* you need to get sober. If you are unable to do this by yourself, call a chemical dependence program in your area. There you can be helped to stop drinking and drugging so you can learn how to prevent relapse.

3. Why did you decide to stop using alcohol and drugs at this time?

   _____

   _____

   _____

   _____

4. Do you want to totally abstain from alcohol and drug use?

☐ Yes ☐ No   Why or why not?

_____

_____

_____

_____

_____

_____

_____

_____

Note: If you have had serious problems with alcohol or drug use, you need to totally abstain from use. This workbook is designed to help you learn how to stay sober and prevent relapse. If you have not made a firm decision to get sober and stay that way, it would be helpful for you to visit with a certified addictions counselor and discuss your objections to setting total abstinence as a goal.

5. How long have you been abstinent? ___ days, ___ months, ___ years

6. Acute withdrawal is a cluster of symptoms which occur when people stop using alcohol or other drugs that they are addicted to. These symptoms usually begin within 24 to 48 hours after stopping alcohol and drug use and persist for a period of three to ten days.

   Are you currently experiencing any of the following symptoms of acute withdrawal?

   ☐ A. rapid heartbeat   ☐ E. confusion

   ☐ B. shortness of breath   ☐ F. hearing noises or seeing things that are not there

   ☐ C. nausea or vomiting   ☐ G. anxiety

   ☐ D. shakiness or tremors   ☐ H. agitation

   Note: If you are experiencing any of the above symptoms you should consult with a doctor who specializes in alcoholism or drug dependence or get an evaluation from a certified addictions counselor. You may need medical treatment to help you recover from acute withdrawal.

7. Post Acute Withdrawal (PAW) is a cluster of symptoms created by the long-term aftereffects of chronic alcohol and drug poisoning to the brain. These symptoms get worse when you are under high stress and gradually improve the longer you are sober and working a recovery program.

Place an "X" in the box in front of the symptoms you are currently experiencing.

☐ A. Difficulty in thinking clearly

☐ B. Difficulty in managing feelings and emotions

☐ C. Difficulty in remembering things

☐ D. Difficulty in sleeping restfully

☐ E. Difficulty with physical coordination and balance

☐ F. Difficulty in managing stress

Note: If you checked any of the above symptoms you should complete the exercise entitled "Post Acute Withdrawal (PAW) Self-Evaluation" (Exercise 4). This exercise will help you evaluate what PAW symptoms you are experiencing and how serious they are.

8. Addictive preoccupation is a cluster of symptoms which occurs in people who are psychologically dependent upon alcohol or other drugs. Most people who are physically addicted are also psychologically dependent.

Place an "X" in the box in front of the symptoms which you are currently experiencing.

☐ A. *Euphoric Recall:* When I think about my past experiences with alcohol and drug use, I tend to remember the good experiences and forget about the bad experiences.

☐ B. *Awfulizing Abstinence:* When I think about what it is like to be abstinent, I tend to think about the bad experiences and forget about the good experiences.

☐ C. *Magical Thinking about Use:* When I think about what would happen if I use alcohol and drugs in the future, I create very positive fantasies in which alcohol and drug use instantly solve many of my problems.

☐ D. *Obsession with Alcohol and Drug Use:* Even though I am abstinent, I find that I can't stop thinking about alcohol and drug use.

☐ E. *Compulsion to Use Alcohol and Drugs:* Even though I am abstinent, I still have a strong desire or urge to use alcohol or drugs.

☐ F. *Craving:* Even though I am abstinent, I still feel a strong physical craving for alcohol and drugs.

Note: If you find that your addictive preoccupation is so strong that you have difficulty thinking about or concentrating on other things, you should talk with a certified alcohol and drug abuse counselor. You may need special counseling to help you turn off these addictive thoughts.

2
Self-Assessment of Treatment Need

Instructions: This exercise will help you determine if you can benefit from relapse prevention therapy (RPT). RPT is designed for people who have recognized and accepted their addiction, made a firm decision to stay abstinent, and have utilized a recovery program to help them stay abstinent. To complete this exercise:

- Read each question and place a check mark in the box in front of the most appropriate answer.

- Refer to the scoring instructions that follow the exercises to determine what your answers mean.

___ 1. How many times have you made serious attempts to stay abstinent?

   ☐ None (0)   ☐ Two (2)   ☐ Four (4)

   ☐ One (1)   ☐ Three (3)   ☐ Five (5)

                                  ☐ More than Five (6)

___ 2. What is the longest period of time that you have been able to stay abstinent?

   ☐ Twelve weeks or more (4)   ☐ Fewer than four weeks (1)

   ☐ Six weeks (3)   ☐ I have never attempted long-term abstinence (0)

   ☐ Four weeks (2)

___ 3. How many times have you been admitted for detoxification from alcohol or drugs?

   ☐ None (0)   ☐ Two (2)   ☐ Four (4)

   ☐ One (1)   ☐ Three (3)   ☐ Five (5)

                                  ☐ More than Five (6)

___ 4. How many times have you left a detoxification program before successfully completing the program?

   ☐ None (0)   ☐ Two (2)   ☐ Four (4)

   ☐ One (1)   ☐ Three (3)   ☐ Five (5)

                                  ☐ More than Five (6)

5. How many times have you been admitted to an inpatient or residential treatment program for alcoholism or drug abuse?

☐ None (0) ☐ Two (2) ☐ Four (4)

☐ One (1) ☐ Three (3) ☐ Five (5)

☐ More than Five (6)

6. How many times have you left one of those inpatient or residential treatment programs before successfully completing the program?

☐ None (0) ☐ Two (2) ☐ Four (4)

☐ One (1) ☐ Three (3) ☐ Five (5)

☐ More than Five (6)

7. How many times have you been admitted to an outpatient treatment program for alcoholism or drug abuse?

☐ None (0) ☐ Two (2) ☐ Four (4)

☐ One (1) ☐ Three (3) ☐ Five (5)

☐ More than Five (6)

8. What is the longest time period that you have been continuously involved in an outpatient or after-care program for chemical dependence?

☐ Sixteen or more weeks (4) ☐ One to four weeks (1)

☐ Nine to sixteen weeks (3) ☐ I have never attended an outpatient/aftercare program. (0)

☐ Five to eight weeks (2)

9. When you were most involved in an outpatient/aftercare program, how many group therapy sessions per month did you attend?

☐ Ten or more per month (4) ☐ Fewer than two per month (1)

☐ Six to nine per month (3) ☐ I have never attended an outpatient / aftercare program. (0)

☐ Two to five per month (2)

10. When you were most actively involved in an outpatient or aftercare program, how many individual therapy sessions did you attend in an average month?

☐ Ten or more per month (4) ☐ Fewer than two per month (1)

☐ Six to nine per month (3) ☐ I have never attended an outpatient / aftercare program. (0)

☐ Two to five per month (2)

___ 11. How many times have you left an outpatient program before successfully completing it?

☐ None (0)   ☐ Two (2)   ☐ Four (4)

☐ One (1)   ☐ Three (3)   ☐ Five (5)

                                        ☐ More than Five (6)

___ 12. When you were most actively involved in your recovery, how many Twelve Step (AA, NA, etc.) meetings per week did you typically attend?

☐ Three or more meetings per week (4)   ☐ Fewer than one meeting per week (1)

☐ Two meetings per week (3)   ☐ I have never attended Twelve Step meetings. (0)

☐ One meeting per week (2)

___ 13. When you were most actively involved in recovery, how many times per week did you have conversations with other recovering people, outside of AA or therapy meetings?

☐ Seven or more times per week (3)   ☐ One to two times per week (1)

☐ Three to six times per week (2)   ☐ Fewer than once per week (0)

___ 14. When you were most actively involved in recovery, how often did you do a tenth-step inventory (i.e., review and evaluate your daily problems and activities outside of AA or therapy meetings)?

☐ Seven or more times per week (3)   ☐ One to two times per week (1)

☐ Three to six times per week (2)   ☐ Fewer than once per week (0)

___ 15. When you were most actively involved in recovery, how often did you read or listen to tapes of recovery-oriented literature or speakers outside of AA and therapy meetings?

☐ Seven or more times per week (3)   ☐ One to two times per week (1)

☐ Three to six times per week (2)   ☐ Fewer than once per week (0)

___ 16. Did you ever have a Twelve Step program sponsor?

☐ Yes (4)   ☐ No (0)

___ 17. When you were most actively involved in recovery, how often did you talk with your Twelve Step program sponsor outside of AA or therapy meetings?

☐ Seven or more times per week (3)   ☐ Fewer than once per week (0)

☐ Three to six times per week (2)   ☐ Did not have a sponsor (0)

☐ One to two times per week (1)

___ 18. Select the statement that most accurately describes your experience with the fourth and fifth steps of AA.

☐ I completed a written fourth step and discussed it with my sponsor. (3)

☐ I completed a written fourth step but did not discuss it with my sponsor. (2)

☐ I did a fourth step in my mind, but never wrote it down or talked with anyone about it. (1)

☐ I never did a fourth or a fifth step. (0)

___ 19. How long after you stopped attending Twelve Step meetings did you return to alcohol and drug use?

☐ I was actively attending meetings when I started using. (5)

☐ Less than one week after I stopped (4)

☐ Between one to three weeks after (3)

☐ Between four to seven weeks after (2)

☐ Eight or more weeks after (1)

___ 20. Select the statement that best describes your understanding and ability to discuss the basic information about chemical dependence.

☐ I can explain it clearly without help. (3)

☐ I can explain it clearly to others with help. (2)

☐ I understand it but cannot explain it. (1)

☐ I do not understand it. (0)

___ 21. Select the statement that best describes how strongly you believe you are suffering from chemical dependence (alcoholism or other drug addictions).

☐ Totally convinced (3)   ☐ Partially convinced (1)

☐ Mostly convinced (2)   ☐ Not convinced (0)

___ 22. Select the statement that best describes the level of pain or inner conflict you experience when you think about or talk about your addiction.

☐ No inner conflict when thinking or talking about addiction. (3)

☐ Mild discomfort when talking about it. (2)

☐ Serious discomfort when talking about it. (1)

☐ So uncomfortable I refuse to talk about it. (0)

____ 23. I am currently sober and experiencing pain or dysfunction.

   ☐ Yes, and I fear that I may relapse soon. (3)

   ☐ Yes, and I have some concern about relapse. (2)

   ☐ Yes, but I am not in immediate danger of relapse but want to lower my risk. (1)

   ☐ No, I am not currently experiencing pain or dysfunction and am not concerned about the immediate risk of relapse. (0)

____ 24. In the past, I have experienced episodes of pain or dysfunction when abstinent from alcohol or drugs.

   ☐ Yes, and it caused me to use alcohol or drugs in spite of my honest desire not to. (3)

   ☐ Yes, and it caused me to feel a compulsion to use alcohol and drugs in spite of my honest desire not to, but I did not use. (2)

   ☐ Yes, and it caused me to think about using alcohol and drugs without feeling a compulsion, and I did not use. (1)

   ☐ I never experienced episodes of dysfunction. (0)

____ 25. In the past, I have experienced progressive problems while abstinent from alcohol and drugs that caused me to think about using alcohol or drugs for relief.

   ☐ Yes, and it caused me to use alcohol or drugs in spite of my honest desire not to. (3)

   ☐ Yes, and it caused me to feel a compulsion to use alcohol and drugs in spite of my honest desire not to, but I did not use. (2)

   ☐ Yes, and it caused me to think about using alcohol and drugs without feeling a compulsion, and I did not use. (1)

   ☐ I never experienced progressive problems. (0)

Scoring and Interpretation

1. A number appears after each answer on the questionnaire. Write that number assigned to the answer that you selected in the space provided in front of the question.

2. Add all of the numbers and write the total score in the space provided.

Total Score = _____

If your score is ...		You probably need ...
0 - 24	_____	Primary Treatment and Twelve Steps
25 - 41	_____	Relapse Prevention, Twelve Steps, and Primary Treatment
41 - 52	_____	Relapse Prevention Therapy

Primary Treatment is designed to help people understand, recognize, and accept their addiction and develop a recovery plan.

Relapse Prevention Therapy is designed to help people understand the relapse process, identify and manage relapse warning signs, and set up a revised recovery program that allows for the identification and management of the warning signs that lead to relapse.

Most people who relapse need to review a number of basic recovery skills and then develop a relapse prevention plan.

3-A
Recovery Program Evaluation

Developed by Terence T. Gorski

Instructions: Please answer the following questions. Think carefully about what you did to manage your recovery during your last efforts to stay sober.

___ 1. How often did you attend group or individual counseling sessions?

☐ Never(0) ☐ Sometimes(1) ☐ Often(2) ☐ Very Often(3)

Please describe the type of counseling you participated in and your personal reaction to that counseling.

_____

_____

_____

_____

_____

___ 2. How often did you regularly attend AA or self-help group meetings?

☐ Never(0) ☐ Sometimes(1) ☐ Often(2) ☐ Very Often(3)

A. How many meetings per week did you attend? ___

B. What type of meetings did you attend?

☐ Open ☐ Closed ☐ Speaker ☐ Discussion

C. Did you have a home group? ☐ Yes ☐ No

D. Please describe your personal reaction to the meetings:

_____

_____

_____

_____

___ 3. How often did you talk with your sponsor in your Twelve Step self-help group (AA, NA, etc.)? If you did not have a sponsor, check never.

☐ Never(0)   ☐ Sometimes(1)   ☐ Often(2)   ☐ Very Often(3)

If you had a sponsor, please describe your relationship with him or her, including the good and bad points of that relationship.

_____

_____

_____

_____

_____

___ 4. The following is a list of the twelve steps of AA. Read each step and place a check in the answer that most clearly describes your past completion of that task.

	Fully Completed	Partially Completed	Did Not Start
Step 1	☐ (2)	☐ (1)	☐ (0)
Step 2	☐ (2)	☐ (1)	☐ (0)
Step 3	☐ (2)	☐ (1)	☐ (0)
Step 4	☐ (2)	☐ (1)	☐ (0)
Step 5	☐ (2)	☐ (1)	☐ (0)
Step 6	☐ (2)	☐ (1)	☐ (0)
Step 7	☐ (2)	☐ (1)	☐ (0)
Step 8	☐ (2)	☐ (1)	☐ (0)
Step 9	☐ (2)	☐ (1)	☐ (0)
Step 10	☐ (2)	☐ (1)	☐ (0)
Step 11	☐ (2)	☐ (1)	☐ (0)
Step 12	☐ (2)	☐ (1)	☐ (0)
Total Points	_____	_____ =	(_____)

Please describe how you felt about working the steps, which steps you found helpful, and which you found not to be helpful.

_____

_____

_____

_____

_____

_____ 5. How frequently did you eat three well-balanced meals per day?

☐ Never(0)　　☐ Sometimes(1)　　☐ Often(2)　　☐ Very Often(3)

Please describe an average daily eating plan.

Breakfast: _____

Morning Snack: _____

Lunch: _____

Afternoon Snack: _____

Dinner: _____

Evening Snack: _____

Other: _____

_____ 6. How often did you eat foods high in sugars (candy, chocolate, cakes, etc.)?

☐ Very Often(0)　　☐ Often(1)　　☐ Sometimes(2)　　☐ Never(3)

Please describe your favorite high sugar or binge foods and how you feel before, during, and after an episode of heavy eating.

_____

_____

_____

_____

_____ 7. How often did you drink beverages containing caffeine?

☐ Very Often(0)　　☐ Often(1)　　☐ Sometimes(2)　　☐ Never(3)

A. How much caffeine would you consume in a normal day?

☐ Cups of coffee　　　　　　　　　　　=　_____.

☐ Cans of caffeinated soft drinks　　　=　_____.

☐ Other (specify): _____　=　_____.

B. How often did you notice a change in mood (becoming more stimulated, energized, alert, or wired) as a result of your use of caffeine?

☐ Never(0)　　☐ Sometimes(1)　　☐ Often(2)　　☐ Very Often(3)

____ 8. How often did you use nicotine (including cigarettes, cigars, and smokeless tobacco)?

☐ Very Often(0)　　☐ Often(1)　　☐ Sometimes(2)　　☐ Never(3)

____ 9. How often did you exercise at least three times per week for a minimum period of 20 to 30 minutes in a manner that was strenuous enough to make you breathe hard and begin to sweat?

☐ Never(0)　　☐ Sometimes(1)　　☐ Often(2)　　☐ Very Often(3)

Please describe your regular exercise habits:

_____

_____

_____

_____

____ 10. How often have you used relaxation techniques?

☐ Never(0)　　☐ Sometimes(1)　　☐ Often(2)　　☐ Very Often(3)

Please check the type and frequency of relaxation exercises that you used.

Type of Relaxation Exercise Used:　　　　　　　　　**Frequency Used:**

	Never	Sometimes	Often	Very Often
1. Breathing exercises	☐	☐	☐	☐
2. Muscle relaxation	☐	☐	☐	☐
3. Guided imagery	☐	☐	☐	☐
4. Conscious relaxation of various parts of your body	☐	☐	☐	☐
5. Biofeedback	☐	☐	☐	☐

____ 11. How often did you use prayer and meditation on a regular basis to help you recover?

☐ Never(0)　　☐ Sometimes(1)　　☐ Often(2)　　☐ Very Often(3)

Please describe the types of prayer and meditation you found most helpful and least helpful:

_____

_____

_____

_____

___ 12. How frequently did you talk with people about your life and ask for feedback on a regular basis?

☐ Never(0)   ☐ Sometimes(1)   ☐ Often(2)   ☐ Very Often(3)

Please describe the primary people you talked to and what you talked to them about:

_____

_____

_____

_____

_____

___ 13. How often did you attempt to solve problems promptly as they came up?

☐ Never(0)   ☐ Sometimes(1)   ☐ Often(2)   ☐ Very Often(3)

A. Please describe the types of problems you attempted to solve promptly as they came up.

_____

_____

_____

_____

_____

B. Please describe the types of problems you tended to put off solving.

_____

_____

_____

_____

_____

___ 14 . How often did you schedule time for recreational activities (recreational activities are activities you consider to be fun)?

☐ Never(0)   ☐ Sometimes(1)   ☐ Often(2)   ☐ Very Often(3)

A. Please describe the recreational activities you enjoyed most.

_____

_____

_____

_____

_____

B. Please describe the recreational activities you least enjoyed and why you didn't enjoy them.

_____

_____

_____

_____

_____

___ 15. How often did you schedule time for activities with your family?

☐ Never(0)   ☐ Sometimes(1)   ☐ Often(2)   ☐ Very Often(3)

Please describe your current relationship with the members of your family. Describe how your addiction and tendency to relapse has affected your relationship with your family.

_____

_____

_____

_____

_____

16. How often did you schedule time to spend with friends?

☐ Never(0) ☐ Sometimes(1) ☐ Often(2) ☐ Very Often(3)

Please list the current friends you have and how close you feel to them:

_____

_____

_____

_____

_____

_____

_____

_____

17. How often did you work on a regular schedule that didn't interfere with recreational or treatment activities?

☐ Never(0) ☐ Sometimes(1) ☐ Often(2) ☐ Very Often(3)

Please describe your typical work week. If you tend to overwork (work more than 8 hours per day or 40 hours per week, please describe how many hours and why you work that hard).

_____

_____

_____

_____

_____

_____

_____

_____

___ 18. How often did you schedule some quiet time to think and plan your recovery program on a regular basis?

☐ Never(0)   ☐ Sometimes(1)   ☐ Often(2)   ☐ Very Often(3)

Please describe your feelings and reactions to planning periods of quiet time for yourself and your recovery:

_____

_____

_____

_____

_____

Scoring And Interpretation Key

The degree to which the lack of recovery support activities contributed to your relapse can be roughly evaluated by counting the number of points scored in answering the above questions. Next to each multiple choice answer is a numeric score. Add all of those scores together and place your total score below.

TOTAL SCORE = _____ out of 75.

The following guidelines will help you interpret the relationship of your basic recovery program to the tendency to relapse. If you scored...

0 - 25 Points: Lack of recovery support activities was probably a primary factor in your relapse.

26 - 50 Points: Lack of recovery support activities was probably a strong influence on your past relapse, but there are probably other areas that need to be considered in terms of stressors, problems, and relapse warning signs.

51 - 75 Points: Other problems probably interfered with the effectiveness of your recovery program.

3-B
Recovery Program Worksheet
Evaluating Strengths and Weaknesses

Strengths in Past Recovery Programs: What things did you do in your past recovery programs that were helpful and can act as a foundation as you plan a new and more effective program?

_____

_____

_____

_____

_____

_____

_____

_____

_____

_____

_____

_____

_____

_____

_____

_____

Weaknesses in Past Recovery Programs: What things did you do or fail to do in your recovery program that weakened you or set you up to relapse?

_____

_____

_____

_____

_____

_____

_____

_____

_____

_____

_____

_____

_____

_____

_____

_____

_____

_____

3-C

Recovery Program Worksheet

Evaluating Levels of Expectancy

1. Did you expect too much of yourself and attempt to do too much too fast in your previous recovery efforts?

    ☐ Yes   ☐ No

    Please explain why you answered the question as you did:

    _____

    _____

    _____

    _____

    _____

2. Did you expect too little of yourself and fail to put into practice the basics of recovery?

    ☐ Yes   ☐ No

    Please explain why you answered the question as you did:

    _____

    _____

    _____

    _____

    _____

    _____

3. Did you attempt to do the wrong kinds of things in your previous recovery efforts? In other words, did you focus on the easy aspects of recovery by doing things that made you look good while avoiding or denying the more difficult aspects of recovery which would address your major problems?

☐ Yes ☐ No

Please explain why you answered the question as you did:

_____

_____

_____

_____

_____

_____

_____

4. Please list the things you will need to do differently in your recovery if you are to avoid relapse in the future.

_____

_____

_____

_____

_____

_____

_____

_____

E X E R C I S E
4
Post Acute Withdrawal (PAW) Self-Evaluation

Developed by Terence T. Gorski

The regular and heavy use of alcohol and other drugs can damage the brain. It can take between six and eighteen months of sobriety for the brain to heal. While the brain is healing it is common for recovering people to experience difficulty in thinking clearly, managing feelings and emotions, remembering things, sleeping restfully, maintaining physical coordination, and managing stress. These symptoms are called Post Acute Withdrawal (PAW). During times of high stress these PAW symptoms can get so bad that they interfere with normal living and working a recovery program. As a result they can increase the risk of relapse.

If you have serious problems with PAW symptoms, you may need special help in completing the relapse prevention exercises in this workbook. The following questions will help you decide if you are having PAW symptoms and how severe they are. If you discover that you are having frequent or disruptive PAW symptoms, set up an appointment with a doctor who understands chemical addictions and a certified alcohol and drug abuse counselor who can help you set up a plan to manage these symptoms.

Instructions: Answer the following questions by checking the one box that is most correct.

Part 1:   **Difficulty in Thinking Clearly**

1-A.   How often do you experience difficulty in thinking clearly?
(Select only one.)

☐ Less than once per week   ☐ Once per day

☐ Once per week   ☐ More than once per day

☐ Several times per week

1-B.   When you have difficulty in thinking clearly, which of the following do you experience?
(Check all that apply.)

☐ I can't concentrate or pay attention for more than a few minutes.

☐ I can't solve problems that I used to be able to solve easily.

☐ I start thinking the same things over and over again and I have a hard time thinking about anything else.

☐ I have a hard time understanding words or ideas unless they describe people or things that I can actually see or touch.

☐ My thoughts contradict each other and I can't seem to think in an orderly or logical way.

☐ I can't see the causes of problems that should be obvious to me.

☐ I can't figure out what is the most important thing to do or set priorities.

☐ I can't predict the logical consequences of my own or other people's behavior even when those consequences should be obvious to me.

☐ I can't take appropriate action based on my judgment and do what I say to myself I need to do.

☐ I can't stop doing things that I know will hurt me or others.

1-C. Which of the following statements most accurately describes the relationship between stress and your difficulties in thinking clearly? (Select only one.)

☐ I only have difficulty in thinking clearly when I am under high stress. During periods of low stress my thinking returns to normal.

☐ I have difficulty thinking clearly during periods of high stress and low stress. It seems like when I am sober I can never think clearly.

1-D. How long does this difficulty in thinking clearly usually last? (Select only one.)

☐ Less than fifteen minutes   ☐ One to three days

☐ Fifteen minutes to one hour   ☐ Four to seven days

☐ One to six hours   ☐ Eight days or longer

☐ Seven to twenty-three hours

1-E. How well do you function during the times when you have difficulty in thinking clearly? (Select only one.)

☐ I can function normally without extra effort.

☐ I can function normally but it takes extra effort.

☐ Sometimes I can't function normally even with extra effort.

☐ Most of the time I can't function normally even with extra effort.

Part 2: Difficulty in Managing Feelings and Emotions

2-A. How often do you have difficulty in managing feelings and emotions? (Select only one.)

☐ Less than once per week   ☐ Once per day

☐ Once per week   ☐ More than once per day

☐ Several times per week

2-B. What feelings do you have the most difficulty in managing? (Select all that apply.)

☐ Strength   ☐ Security   ☐ Weakness   ☐ Fear

☐ Anger   ☐ Fulfillment   ☐ Caring   ☐ Frustration

☐ Joy   ☐ Guilt   ☐ Sorrow   ☐ Shame

2-C. When you have difficulty in managing feelings and emotions which of the following do you experience? (Select only one.)

☐ I emotionally overreact (the feelings I have are stronger than I believe they should be considering the problem I am having or the situation I am in).

☐ I feel emotionally numb (I don't know what I am feeling).

☐ I shift between emotional overreaction and emotional numbness.

☐ I am able to tell other people what I am feeling when it is appropriate or important to do so.

2-D. Which of the following statements most accurately describes the relationship between stress and your difficulties in managing feelings and emotions? (Select only one.)

☐ I only have difficulty in managing feelings and emotions when I am under very high stress. During periods of low stress my emotions return to normal.

☐ I have difficulty managing feelings and emotions during periods of high stress and low stress. It seems like when I am sober I can never manage my feelings.

2-E. How long does this difficulty in managing feelings and emotions usually last? (Select only one.)

☐ Less that fifteen minutes   ☐ One to three days

☐ Fifteen minutes to one hour   ☐ Four to seven days

☐ One to six hours   ☐ Eight days or longer

☐ Seven to twenty-three hours

2-F. How well do you function during the times when you have difficulty managing your feelings and emotions? (Select only one.)

☐ I can function normally without extra effort.

☐ I can function normally but it takes extra effort.

☐ Sometimes I can't function normally even with extra effort.

☐ Most of the time I can't function normally even with extra effort.

Part 3: Difficulty Remembering Things

3-A. How often do you have difficulty remembering things? (Select only one.)

☐ Less than once per week   ☐ Once per day

☐ Once per week   ☐ More than once per day

☐ Several times per week

3-B. When you have difficulty in remembering things, which of the following do you experience? (Check all that apply.)

☐ I forget things that I learn shortly after I learn them.

☐ I am not able to remember things that I knew before.

☐ I am not able to remember important childhood events.

☐ I am not able to remember important adulthood events.

3-C. Which of the following statements most accurately describes the relationship between stress and your difficulties in remembering things? (Select only one.)

☐ I only have difficulty in remembering things when I am under very high stress. During periods of low stress, my ability to remember returns to normal.

☐ I have difficulty remembering things during periods of high stress and low stress. It seems like when I am sober I can never remember things.

3-D. How long does this difficulty in remembering things usually last? (Select only one.)

☐ Less that fifteen minutes   ☐ One to three days

☐ Fifteen minutes to one hour   ☐ Four to seven days

☐ One to six hours   ☐ Eight days or longer

☐ Seven to twenty-three hours

3-E. How well do you function during the times when you have difficulty remembering things? (Select only one.)

☐ I can function normally without extra effort.

☐ I can function normally but it takes extra effort.

☐ Sometimes I can't function normally even with extra effort.

☐ Most of the time I can't function normally even with extra effort.

Part 4:   **Difficulty with Physical Coordination**

4-A. How often do you have difficulty with physical coordination? (Select only one.)

☐ Less than once per week   ☐ Once per day

☐ Once per week   ☐ More than once per day

☐ Several times per week

4-B. When you have difficulty with physical coordination which of the following do you experience? (Select all that apply.)

☐ Dizziness   ☐ Slow reflexes

☐ Trouble with balance   ☐ Clumsiness

☐ Hand-eye coordination problems   ☐ Accident proneness

4-C. Which of the following statements most accurately describes the relationship between stress and your difficulties with physical coordination? (Select only one.)

☐ I only have difficulty with physical coordination when I am under very high stress. During periods of low stress, my physical coordination returns to normal.

☐ I have difficulty with physical coordination during periods of high stress and low stress. It seems like when I am sober I always have difficulty with physical coordination.

4-D. How well do you function during the times when you have difficulty with physical coordination? (Select only one.)

☐ I can function normally without extra effort.

☐ I can function normally but it takes extra effort.

☐ Sometimes I can't function normally even with extra effort.

☐ Most of the time I can't function normally even with extra effort.

Part 5:   Difficulty in Sleeping Restfully

5-A.   How often do you experience difficulty in sleeping restfully? (Select only one.)

☐ Less than once per week   ☐ Once per day

☐ Once per week   ☐ More than once per day

☐ Several times per week

5-B.   When you have difficulty in sleeping restfully, which of the following do you experience?
(Select all that apply.)

☐ Difficulty in falling asleep   ☐ Always feeling tired

☐ Unusual or disturbing dreams   ☐ Changes in time of day when sleep occurs

☐ Awaking many times during the night   ☐ Sleeping for extremely long periods

☐ Not being rested after sleeping   ☐ None of the above

5-C.   Which of the following statements most accurately describes the relationship between stress and
your difficulties in sleeping restfully? (Select only one.)

☐ I only have difficulty in sleeping restfully when I am under very high stress. During periods
of low stress, my sleeping returns to normal.

☐ I have difficulty sleeping restfully during periods of high stress and low stress. It seems like
when I am sober I can never sleep restfully.

5-D.   How long does this difficulty with sleeping restfully usually last? (Select only one.)

☐ Less than one night   ☐ Four to seven nights

☐ One to three nights   ☐ Eight nights or longer

5-E.   How well do you function during the times when you have difficulty sleeping restfully?
(Select only one.)

☐ I can function normally without extra effort.

☐ I can function normally but it takes extra effort.

☐ Sometimes I can't function normally even with extra effort.

☐ Most of the time I can't function normally even with extra effort.

Part 6:　**Difficulty in Managing Stress**

6-A.　How often do you experience difficulty in managing stress? (Select only one.)

☐ Less than once per week　　　☐ Once per day

☐ Once per week　　　☐ More than once per day

☐ Several times per week

6-B.　When you have difficulty managing stress, which of the following do you experience?
(Select all that apply.)

☐ Inability to recognize minor signs of stress

☐ Inability to relax when stress is recognized

☐ Constant fatigue or weariness

☐ Fear of physical collapse due to stress

☐ Fear of mental collapse due to stress

☐ Inability to function normally due to severe stress

6-C.　Which of the following statements most accurately describes the relationship between stress and
your difficulties in managing stress? (Select only one.)

☐ I only have difficulty in managing stress when I am under very high stress. During periods
of low stress, my ability to manage stress returns to normal.

☐ I have difficulty managing stress during periods of high stress and low stress. It seems like
when I am sober I can never manage stress.

6-D.　How long does this difficulty with managing stress usually last? (Select only one.)

☐ Less than one day　　　☐ Four to seven days

☐ One to three days　　　☐ Eight days or longer

6-E.　How well do you function during the times when you have difficulty managing stress?
(Select only one.)

☐ I can function normally without extra effort.

☐ I can function normally but it takes extra effort.

☐ Sometimes I can't function normally even with extra effort.

☐ Most of the time I can't function normally even with extra effort.

5
Immediate Relapse Prevention Plan

Developed by Terence T. Gorski

Instructions: Before you begin developing a comprehensive relapse prevention plan, it is important to take some immediate steps to identify the problems or situations which can cause you to relapse within the next six weeks and develop plans for coping with them. These exercises will ask you to identify three situations that can put you at risk of relapsing during the next six weeks. They will then ask you to identify the thoughts, feelings, and actions that you used in that situation that set you up to relapse.

A high-risk situation is any experience that puts you at risk of using alcohol or drugs. Examples of high-risk situations may be: (1) having dinner in a restaurant that serves drinks, (2) going back to work where you will have to deal with co-workers who you used to drink with, or (3) dealing with angry customers at work. Any situation that creates a strong temptation to use alcohol or drugs to cope with it is a high-risk situation.

E X E R C I S E
5-A
Telephone Contacts

Instructions: List the names and telephone numbers of five people you can call if you feel an urge to start addictive use who will support you in staying in recovery. (Be sure to list two people you can call at night.)

1.   Name: _____ Home phone: _____

   Available: ☐ Day ☐ Evening ☐ Night Work phone: _____

2.   Name: _____ Home phone: _____

   Available: ☐ Day ☐ Evening ☐ Night Work phone: _____

3.   Name: _____ Home phone: _____

   Available: ☐ Day ☐ Evening ☐ Night Work phone: _____

4.   Name: _____ Home phone: _____

   Available: ☐ Day ☐ Evening ☐ Night Work phone: _____

5.   Name: _____ Home phone: _____

   Available: ☐ Day ☐ Evening ☐ Night Work phone: _____

E X E R C I S E
5-B
Immediate High-Risk Situations

Instructions: List three situations that you may be involved in within the next several weeks that could cause you to feel like starting addictive use.

1. Immediate High-Risk Situation #1:

_____

_____

_____

_____

2. Immediate High-Risk Situation #2:

_____

_____

_____

_____

3. Immediate High-Risk Situation #3:

_____

_____

_____

_____

5-C
Immediate Relapse Prevention Plan #1

1. **Immediate High-Risk Situation #1:** Describe a situation that could put you in risk of relapse which could occur within the next six weeks.

    _____

    _____

    _____

    _____

    _____

2. **Irrational Thoughts:** What thoughts are you likely to think in this situation which could cause you to relapse?

    _____

    _____

    _____

    _____

3. **Unmanageable Feelings:** What feelings are you likely to have in this situation which could cause you to relapse?

    _____

    _____

    _____

    _____

4.   **Self-defeating Action Urges:** What are you likely to have an urge to do in this situation which could cause you to relapse?

_____

_____

_____

_____

5.   **More Effective Ways of Thinking:** What is another way to think about this situation that can help you stay sober and avoid relapse?

_____

_____

_____

_____

6.   **More Effective Ways of Managing Your Feelings:** What is another way to manage your feelings in this situation that can help you stay sober and avoid relapse?

_____

_____

_____

_____

7.   **More Effective Ways of Acting:** What is another way of acting in this situation that can help you stay sober and avoid relapse?

_____

_____

_____

_____

5-D
Immediate Relapse Prevention Plan #2

1. **Immediate High-Risk Situation #2:** Describe a situation that could put you in risk of relapse which could occur within the next six weeks.

_____

_____

_____

_____

_____

2. **Irrational Thoughts:** What thoughts are you likely to think in this situation which could cause you to relapse?

_____

_____

_____

_____

3. **Unmanageable Feelings:** What feelings are you likely to have in this situation which could cause you to relapse?

_____

_____

_____

_____

4. **Self-defeating Action Urges:** What are you likely to have an urge to do in this situation which could cause you to relapse?

_____

_____

_____

_____

5. **More Effective Ways of Thinking:** What is another way to think about this situation that can help you stay sober and avoid relapse?

_____

_____

_____

_____

6. **More Effective Ways of Managing Your Feelings:** What is another way to manage your feelings in this situation that can help you stay sober and avoid relapse?

_____

_____

_____

_____

7. **More Effective Ways of Acting:** What is another way of acting in this situation that can help you stay sober and avoid relapse?

_____

_____

_____

_____

5-E
Immediate Relapse Prevention Plan #3

1. **Immediate High-Risk Situation #3:** Describe a situation that could put you in risk of relapse which could occur within the next six weeks.

_____

_____

_____

_____

_____

2. **Irrational Thoughts:** What thoughts are you likely to think in this situation which could cause you to relapse?

_____

_____

_____

_____

3. **Unmanageable Feelings:** What feelings are you likely to have in this situation which could cause you to relapse?

_____

_____

_____

_____

4. **Self-defeating Action Urges:** What are you likely to have an urge to do in this situation which could cause you to relapse?

_____

_____

_____

_____

5. **More Effective Ways of Thinking:** What is another way to think about this situation that can help you stay sober and avoid relapse?

_____

_____

_____

_____

6. **More Effective Ways of Managing Your Feelings:** What is another way to manage your feelings in this situation that can help you stay sober and avoid relapse?

_____

_____

_____

_____

7. **More Effective Ways of Acting:** What is another way of acting in this situation that can help you stay sober and avoid relapse?

_____

_____

_____

_____

6

Relapse Early Intervention Worksheet

Developed by Terence T. Gorski

Instructions: Many recovering people mistakenly believe that if they relapse they have no choice but to keep using addictively until they destroy everything they have gained and hit bottom again. This is not true. With proper planning and preparation, you and those you love can take positive actions to end relapse early, before you hit bottom. This process is called relapse early intervention. To develop an early relapse intervention plan, you do the following:

A. Think about what you could do if you start drinking or drugging that would cause you to stop. This could include things like calling your Twelve Step sponsor, checking into a treatment center, or calling your counselor. Write out the things that you can do to stop a relapse early should it occur.

B. When addicts begin to use substances addictively they are often out of control. Loss of control means that you cannot regulate your thinking, judgment, or behavior. As a result, you cannot stop drinking and drugging by yourself. The good news is that other people can do things to help you stop addictive use and get back in control. The second question asks you to write all of the things that other people can say or do that would motivate you to stop drinking or drugging if you should relapse.

C. Addiction is a disease of denial. When using alcohol or drugs, addicts are able to rationalize and resist nearly anything. As a result they can sabotage the ability of others to help them. The third question asks you to think about how you are likely to attempt to sabotage the efforts of other people who are trying to help you to stop drinking and drugging. Write down advice or recommendations as to how they can effectively help you stop drinking and drugging if you try to refuse their help.

1. If you return to addictive use, what actions can you take to get back into recovery?

_____

_____

_____

_____

_____

_____

_____

_____

2. What actions can others take to encourage you to stop addictive use should you relapse?

_____

_____

_____

_____

_____

_____

_____

3. If you returned to addictive use and others attempted to get you into treatment and you refused, what do you believe would be the most effective strategies for getting you into treatment even if you didn't want to go?

_____

_____

_____

_____

_____

_____

_____

It is strongly recommended that you give a copy of this form to your counselor, family doctor, personal attorney, Twelve Step program sponsor, family members, and other members of your relapse prevention network.

E X E R C I S E
7
Challenging Relapse Justifications

Instructions: Before people return to addictive use they convince themselves that it is reasonable, safe, or justifiable that they do so. In AA this form of thinking is called "stinking thinking." Cognitive therapists call it irrational thinking. The irrational thoughts that you use to convince yourself that it is okay to use alcohol or other drugs are called relapse justifications.

Relapse justifications are things we say to ourselves that convince us that it is okay to use alcohol or drugs. A typical relapse justification begins with a justification and ends with a decision to use. Here are some typical relapse justifications:

1.   I can never relax and enjoy myself sober, so I might as well drink.

2.   I am having worse problems with my spouse since I got sober, so I might as well start drinking and drugging again.

3.   My boss still doesn't trust me even though I have been sober all of these months, so I might as well start using again.

Review your past relapse episodes. Think back to the time just before you decided to start drinking and drugging again. See if you can identify exactly what you said to yourself to justify your decision to drink or drug.

Identify three common relapse justifications and then ask yourself how you can challenge that relapse justification and convince yourself to stay sober.

7-A
Challenging Relapse Justification #1

Relapse Justification #1: I can convince myself that I am justified in using alcohol and drugs by saying to myself...

_____

_____

_____

_____

_____

_____

_____

Challenge #1: I can challenge this relapse justification and convince myself to stay sober by saying to myself...

_____

_____

_____

_____

_____

_____

_____

7-B
Challenging Relapse Justification #2

Relapse Justification #2: I can convince myself that I am justified in using alcohol and drugs by saying to myself...

_____

_____

_____

_____

_____

_____

_____

Challenge #2: I can challenge this relapse justification and convince myself to stay sober by saying to myself...

_____

_____

_____

_____

_____

_____

_____

7-C
Challenging Relapse Justification #3

Relapse Justification #3: I can convince myself that I am justified in using alcohol and drugs by saying to myself...

_____

_____

_____

_____

_____

_____

_____

Challenge #3: I can challenge this relapse justification and convince myself to stay sober by saying to myself...

_____

_____

_____

_____

_____

_____

_____

_____

8-A
Life and Addiction History
Worksheet

Instructions: Many people relapse because they have recurrent life problems that they never learn to cope with. The purpose of completing a life and addiction history is to identify the pattern of recurrent problems that set you up to relapse.

The following exercise will help you to think about your life and how you used alcohol or drugs to help you cope with life problems.

This exercise will ask you questions about:

- Early Childhood (the period between the time you were born and the time you started grammar school)
- Grammar School
- High School
- College (if you attended)
- Military (if you served)
- Adult Work History
- Adult Love History
- Adult Friendship History

1. **Early Childhood:** Describe your early childhood by answering the following questions based upon how you remember your family before you started grammar school.

    A. What kind of a person was your mother?

    _____

    _____

    _____

    _____

    B. What kind of person was your father?

    _____

    _____

    _____

    _____

C. What kind of relationship did your mother and father have?

_____

_____

_____

_____

_____

D. How did you get along with your mother?

_____

_____

_____

_____

_____

E. How did you get along with your father?

_____

_____

_____

_____

_____

F. How did you get along with your brothers and sisters?

_____

_____

_____

_____

G. Describe yourself as a child.

_____

_____

_____

_____

H. What were your primary strengths or good points as a child?

_____

_____

_____

_____

I. What were your primary weaknesses or bad points as a child?

_____

_____

_____

_____

J. What things did you learn that you had to do in order to be a good person?

_____

_____

_____

K. What did you learn that you couldn't do if you wanted to be a good person?

_____

_____

_____

_____

2. **Addictive Use during Childhood:** Children learn important lessons from observing how parents, other family members, and friends of the family use alcohol and drugs. Think back to your childhood and answer these questions based on what you learned from these examples.

A. How often did your mother and father use alcohol or other drugs?

_____

_____

B. When your mother and father used alcohol or other drugs, how much did they tend to use?

_____

_____

C. What did you believe that alcohol or drugs would allow you to do or be when you grew up that you couldn't do or be as a child?

_____

_____

_____

_____

_____

D. What did you believe that alcohol or drugs would allow you to *stop* doing, escape from, or cope with as an adult that you couldn't as a child?

_____

_____

_____

_____

_____

3. **Grammar School:**

A. What positive or good things did you learn about yourself in grammar school?

_____

_____

_____

_____

B. What negative or bad things did you learn about yourself in grammar school?

_____

_____

_____

_____

C. What things did you learn about yourself in grammar school that were the same as what your parents taught you about yourself?

_____

_____

_____

_____

D. What things did you learn about yourself in grammar school that were different from what your parents taught you about yourself?

_____

_____

_____

_____

4. **Addictive Use during Grammar School:**

A. How much alcohol or other drugs did you use?

_____

_____

B. How often did you use alcohol or other drugs?

_____

_____

C. What did you believe that alcohol or drugs would allow you to do or be that you couldn't do or be when not using?

_____

_____

_____

_____

_____

D. What did you believe that alcohol or drugs would allow you to *stop* doing, escape from, or cope with that you couldn't when not using?

_____

_____

_____

_____

_____

5. **High School:**

A. What positive or good things did you learn about yourself in high school?

_____

_____

_____

_____

B. What negative or bad things did you learn about yourself in high school?

_____

_____

_____

_____

C. What things did you learn about yourself in high school that were the same as what your parents taught you about yourself as a child?

_____

_____

_____

_____

D. What things did you learn about yourself in high school that were different from what your parents taught you about yourself as a child?

_____

_____

_____

_____

6. **Addictive Use during High School:**

A. How much alcohol or other drugs did you use?

_____

_____

B. How often did you use alcohol or other drugs?

_____

_____

C. What did you believe that alcohol or drugs would allow you to do or be that you couldn't when not using?

_____

_____

_____

D. What did you believe that alcohol or drugs would allow you to *stop* doing, escape from, or cope with that you couldn't when not using?

_____

_____

_____

E. What benefits did you actually get from alcohol and drug use?

_____

_____

F. What problems did alcohol or drug use cause?

_____

_____

7. **College:**

   A. What positive or good things did you learn about yourself in college?

   _____

   _____

   _____

   _____

   _____

   B. What negative or bad things did you learn about yourself in college?

   _____

   _____

   _____

   _____

   C. What things did you learn about yourself in college that were the same as what your parents taught you about yourself as a child?

   _____

   _____

   _____

   _____

   D. What things did you learn about yourself in college that were different from what your parents taught you about yourself as a child?

   _____

   _____

   _____

   _____

8. **Addictive Use during College:**

A. How much alcohol or other drugs did you use?

_____

_____

B. How often did you use alcohol or other drugs?

_____

_____

C. What did you believe that alcohol or drugs would allow you to do or be that you couldn't when not using?

_____

_____

_____

D. What did you believe that alcohol or drugs would allow you to *stop* doing, escape from, or cope with that you couldn't when not using?

_____

_____

_____

E. What benefits did you actually get from alcohol and drug use?

_____

_____

_____

F. What problems did alcohol or drug use cause?

_____

_____

9. **Military:**

A. What positive or good things did you learn about yourself in the military?

_____

_____

_____

B. What negative or bad things did you learn about yourself in the military?

_____

_____

_____

C. What things did you learn about yourself in the military that were the same as what your parents taught you about yourself as a child?

_____

_____

_____

D. What things did you learn about yourself in the military that were different from what your parents taught you about yourself as a child?

_____

_____

_____

E. Did you serve in a combat area? ☐ Yes   ☐ No

F. Have you experienced any problems as a result of your experiences in combat areas? ☐ Yes   ☐ No

If yes, briefly describe the problems: _____

_____

10. **Addictive Use during the Military:**

A. How much alcohol or other drugs did you use?

_____

_____

B. How often did you use alcohol or other drugs?

_____

_____

C. What did you believe that alcohol or drugs would allow you to do or be that you couldn't do or be when not using?

_____

_____

_____

D. What did you believe that alcohol or drugs would allow you to *stop* doing, escape from, or cope with that you couldn't do or escape from when not using?

_____

_____

_____

E. What benefits did you actually get from alcohol and drug use?

_____

_____

_____

F. What problems did alcohol or drug use cause?

_____

_____

_____

11. **Adult Work:** List the jobs you have held since starting to work, how long you worked at each job, and why you left.

_____

_____

_____

_____

_____

_____

_____

_____

_____

_____

_____

_____

_____

_____

_____

_____

_____

_____

_____

12. **The Impact of Addictive Use upon Work:**

A. What did alcohol or drugs allow you to do or be on the job that you couldn't do or be sober?

_____

_____

_____

_____

_____

B. What did alcohol or drugs allow you to *stop* doing or being or allow you to escape from on the job that you couldn't sober?

_____

_____

_____

_____

_____

C. What were the consequences of your alcohol and drug use upon your work history?

_____

_____

_____

_____

_____

13. **Adult Family / Intimate:** List your intimate, sexual, and love relationships that you have had, how long each lasted, and why each relationship ended.

_____

_____

_____

_____

_____

_____

_____

_____

_____

_____

_____

_____

_____

_____

_____

_____

_____

_____

14. The Impact of Addictive Use upon Family / Intimate Life:

A. What did alcohol or drugs allow you to do or be intimately that you couldn't do or be sober?

_____

_____

_____

_____

_____

B. What intimate obligations or pressures did alcohol or drugs allow you to *stop* doing, escape from, or cope with that you couldn't sober?

_____

_____

_____

_____

_____

C. What were the consequences of your alcohol and drug use upon your intimate and family life?

_____

_____

_____

_____

_____

15. **Adult Social / Friendship:** List your nonsexual, close personal friendships with members of the same and opposite sex that you have had, how long each lasted, and why each relationship ended.

_____

_____

_____

_____

_____

_____

_____

_____

_____

_____

_____

_____

_____

_____

_____

_____

_____

_____

_____

_____

16. **The Impact of Addictive Use upon Social Life and Friendships:**

A. What did alcohol or drugs allow you to do or be with your friends that you couldn't do or be sober?

_____

_____

_____

_____

_____

B. What social obligations or pressures did alcohol or drugs allow you to *stop* doing or being or allow you to escape from that you couldn't sober?

_____

_____

_____

_____

_____

C. What were the consequences of your alcohol and drug use upon your social life and friendships?

_____

_____

_____

_____

_____

17. In what ways have you turned out like your parents believed that you would when you were a child?

_____

_____

_____

_____

_____

_____

_____

_____

18. In what ways have you become different than your parents thought that you would become as a child?

_____

_____

_____

_____

_____

_____

_____

_____

19. The positive things that I used to believe alcohol or drugs would allow me to do or become in my life are...

_____

_____

_____

_____

_____

_____

_____

20. The things that I used to believe that alcohol or drugs could help me *stop* doing, escape from, or cope with are....

_____

_____

_____

_____

_____

_____

_____

_____

_____

E X E R C I S E
8-B
Life and Addiction History
Documentation Form

Instructions: Summarize your life and addiction history in the spaces below. Look for the relationship between what was happening in your life and how you used your addiction to cope with what was happening.

Life History:

1.   **Childhood:**

_____

_____

_____

_____

_____

_____

3.   **Grammar School:**

_____

_____

_____

_____

Alcohol and Drug History:

2.   **Addictive Use:**

_____

_____

_____

_____

_____

_____

4.   **Addictive Use:**

_____

_____

_____

_____

5.   **High School:**

_____

_____

_____

_____

_____

_____

6.   **Addictive Use:**

_____

_____

_____

_____

_____

_____

7.   **College:**

_____

_____

_____

_____

_____

_____

8.   **Addictive Use:**

_____

_____

_____

_____

_____

_____

9.   **Military:**

_____

_____

_____

_____

_____

10.   **Addictive Use:**

_____

_____

_____

_____

_____

11.   **Adult Work:**

_____

_____

_____

_____

_____

_____

12.   **Addictive Use:**

_____

_____

_____

_____

_____

_____

13.   **Adult Family / Intimate:**

_____

_____

_____

_____

_____

14.   **Addictive Use:**

_____

_____

_____

_____

_____

15.   **Adult Social:**

_____

_____

_____

_____

_____

16.   **Addictive Use:**

_____

_____

_____

_____

_____

17. **Similarities to Parental Expectations:**

_____

_____

_____

_____

18. **Differences from Parental Expectations:**

_____

_____

_____

_____

19. **What I used to believe alcohol or drugs would allow me to do or become in my life:**

_____

_____

_____

_____

20. **What I used to believe alcohol or drugs could help me stop doing, escape from, or cope with:**

_____

_____

_____

_____

9-A

The Relapse Calendar

Developed by Terence T. Gorski, 1988

Many relapse-prone people minimize or "awfulize" their memories of relapse. Those who minimize say to themselves, "I seldom relapse and when I do it isn't very bad at all." Those who awfulize say to themselves, "I have relapsed so many times I couldn't even count them, and when I do relapse I always lose everything."

The Relapse Calendar will help you remember how many relapse episodes you have had, what caused them to begin, and how long they lasted. A relapse episode is a period of time when you used alcohol or drugs that was followed by at least ten days of abstinence.

Instructions:

1.   Enter the date of your first serious attempt at abstinence in the space indicated on the first line.

2.   The first column gives you a place to enter years. Starting with the year of your first serious attempt at abstinence, enter all the successive years down to the present.

3.   Following each year is a time line divided by months. Locate the date of your first serious attempt at abstinence on the time line and mark it with a hash mark (I).

4.   Identify the point on the time line when you returned to addictive use. Place another hash mark (I) at that point on the time line. Connect the two hash marks with a solid line to represent this first period of abstinence.

5.   Identify the next point on the time line when you became abstinent and mark it with a hash mark. Connect that with the previous hash mark using a jagged line (/\/\/\) to indicate this period of addictive use.

6.   Mark all periods of abstinence with solid lines and all periods of addictive use with jagged lines. Be sure to include all periods of abstinence and all relapse episodes.

The Relapse Calendar

Developed by Terence T. Gorski, 1988

First Serious Attempt at Abstinence: _____

Year	Jan	Feb	Mar	Apr	May	June	July	Aug	Sept	Oct	Nov	Dec

Year	Jan	Feb	Mar	Apr	May	June	July	Aug	Sept	Oct	Nov	Dec

9-B
The Relapse Episode List

Developed by Terence T. Gorski, 1988

Instructions: The purpose of completing the relapse episode list is to help you think about each period of abstinence and relapse in more detail. In completing the following instructions, refer back to your relapse calendar.

1. Enter the date of your first serious attempt at abstinence in the space indicated on the first line.

2. Think of your first period of abstinence and give it a title that describes what that period of abstinence meant to you.

    Example 1: If you stopped addictive use to keep your spouse from getting a divorce, an appropriate title would be "Save My Marriage."

    Example 2: If you quit addictive use to keep from being fired, a good title would be "Save My Job."

    Example 3: If you quit because you felt too physically ill to keep using, a good title would be "Too Sick to Keep Using."

3. Enter the date your first period of abstinence began in the box marked "Start Date."

4. Enter the date you returned to addictive use in the box marked "Stop Date."

5. Enter the length of time you were abstinent in the box marked "Duration."

6. Think of your first relapse episode and give it a title that describes what that relapse meant to you.

    Example 1: If you relapsed because your spouse divorced you even though you stopped drinking, a good title would be "The Divorce Relapse."

    Example 2: If you relapsed because you were fired or laid off in spite of being abstinent, a good title would be "The Job Loss Relapse."

7. Enter the date your first relapse episode began in the box marked "Start Date."

8. Enter the date you stopped addictive use and returned to abstinence in the box marked "Stop Date."

9. Enter the length of time you were using addictively in the box marked "Duration."

(Continued)

10. Think about how much damage was done by this first relapse episode.

A. If the relapse caused you minor personal problems that did not affect others or create serious consequences, place a check mark in the box in front of "Mild."

B. If the relapse caused problems for others but did not create serious damage to your health or life-style, place a check mark in the box in front of "Moderate."

C. If the relapse resulted in serious problems to others, to your health, or to your life-style, place a check mark in the box in front of "Severe." Mark severe if...

1. You needed to be hospitalized for detoxification or medical problems,

2. You were put under corrective discipline, suspended, or terminated from employment as a result of the relapse,

3. You were separated or divorced as a result of the relapse,

4. You were arrested as a result of the relapse.

11. Repeat steps two through ten for each period of abstinence and relapse on your Relapse Calendar.

The Relapse Episode List

Developed by Terence T. Gorski, 1988

My First Serious Attempt at Abstinence Started on: _____

Abstinence Period #1: Title	Start Date	Stop Date	Duration

Relapse Episode #1: Title	Start Date	Stop Date	Duration

Severity of Consequences:	☐ Mild - Minor Personal Problems
	☐ Moderate - Problems to Others, No Serious Damage
	☐ Severe - Damage to Others, Health, and Life-style

Abstinence Period #2: Title	Start Date	Stop Date	Duration

Relapse Episode #2: Title	Start Date	Stop Date	Duration

Severity of Consequences:	☐ Mild - Minor Personal Problems
	☐ Moderate - Problems to Others, No Serious Damage
	☐ Severe - Damage to Others, Health, and Life-style

Abstinence Period #3: Title	Start Date	Stop Date	Duration

Relapse Episode #3: Title	Start Date	Stop Date	Duration

Severity of Consequences:	☐ Mild - Minor Personal Problems
	☐ Moderate - Problems to Others, No Serious Damage
	☐ Severe - Damage to Others, Health, and Life-style

Abstinence Period #4: Title	Start Date	Stop Date	Duration

Relapse Episode #4: Title	Start Date	Stop Date	Duration

Severity of Consequences:	☐ Mild - Minor Personal Problems
	☐ Moderate - Problems to Others, No Serious Damage
	☐ Severe - Damage to Others, Health, and Life-style

Abstinence Period #5: Title	Start Date	Stop Date	Duration

Relapse Episode #5: Title	Start Date	Stop Date	Duration

Severity of Consequences:	☐ Mild - Minor Personal Problems ☐ Moderate - Problems to Others, No Serious Damage ☐ Severe - Damage to Others, Health, and Life-style

Abstinence Period #6: Title	Start Date	Stop Date	Duration

Relapse Episode #6: Title	Start Date	Stop Date	Duration

Severity of Consequences:	☐ Mild - Minor Personal Problems ☐ Moderate - Problems to Others, No Serious Damage ☐ Severe - Damage to Others, Health, and Life-style

Abstinence Period #7: Title	Start Date	Stop Date	Duration

Relapse Episode #7: Title	Start Date	Stop Date	Duration

Severity of Consequences:	☐ Mild - Minor Personal Problems ☐ Moderate - Problems to Others, No Serious Damage ☐ Severe - Damage to Others, Health, and Life-style

Abstinence Period #8: Title	Start Date	Stop Date	Duration

Relapse Episode #8: Title	Start Date	Stop Date	Duration

Severity of Consequences:	☐ Mild - Minor Personal Problems ☐ Moderate - Problems to Others, No Serious Damage ☐ Severe - Damage to Others, Health, and Life-style

Abstinence Period #9: Title	Start Date	Stop Date	Duration

Relapse Episode #9: Title	Start Date	Stop Date	Duration

Severity of Consequences:	☐ Mild - Minor Personal Problems ☐ Moderate - Problems to Others, No Serious Damage ☐ Severe - Damage to Others, Health, and Life-style

Abstinence Period #10: Title	Start Date	Stop Date	Duration
Relapse Episode #10: Title	Start Date	Stop Date	Duration

Severity of Consequences:	☐ Mild	-	Minor Personal Problems
	☐ Moderate	-	Problems to Others, No Serious Damage
	☐ Severe	-	Damage to Others, Health, and Life-style

Abstinence Period #11: Title	Start Date	Stop Date	Duration
Relapse Episode #11: Title	Start Date	Stop Date	Duration

Severity of Consequences:	☐ Mild	-	Minor Personal Problems
	☐ Moderate	-	Problems to Others, No Serious Damage
	☐ Severe	-	Damage to Others, Health, and Life-style

Abstinence Period #12: Title	Start Date	Stop Date	Duration
Relapse Episode #12: Title	Start Date	Stop Date	Duration

Severity of Consequences:	☐ Mild	-	Minor Personal Problems
	☐ Moderate	-	Problems to Others, No Serious Damage
	☐ Severe	-	Damage to Others, Health, and Life-style

E X E R C I S E
9-C
Relapse Episode Analysis

Developed by Terence T. Gorski, 1988

Instructions: The purpose of relapse episode analysis is to describe in detail some important information about your three most recent periods of abstinence and relapse.

1. Enter the Title, Start Date, Stop Date, and Duration for your most recent period of abstinence by copying it from your Relapse Episode List.

2. Write a brief description of that period of abstinence.

    Example #1: "Things got better but I was bored and wanted some excitement."

    Example #2: "Things were okay, working a lot, problems at home that I didn't like."

3. Write what you believe your primary setups for relapse were. In other words, what did you do that set you up to return to addictive use?

    Example #1: "I stopped going to meetings and talking to my sponsor because they were asking me to do things I didn't want to do."

    Example #2: "I didn't really think I was addicted because I got well so fast and didn't have cravings. I hung out with friends who were drinking and using."

4. Mark the stage of recovery you were in during this period of abstinence. Use the following guidelines:

    - **Transition:** "I never really believed that I was addicted or needed to abstain. I thought I would be able to control it."

    - **Stabilization:** "I stopped addictive use but always felt agitated, confused, and uneasy. Even though I was abstinent I never felt good or saw things start to get better."

    - **Early Recovery:** "Even though I stopped addictive use and stabilized, I still continued to think, feel, and act in the ways I used to when I was using addictively. I resented being told I had to change."

    - **Middle Recovery:** "I changed my ways of thinking, feeling, and acting, but I never made amends or attempted to fix the problems that my addiction caused to other people and my life-style."

    - **Late Recovery:** "I fixed the damage done to others and my life-style by the addiction, but I never examined or attempted to change the habits that I learned as a child that prevented me from being truly comfortable in sobriety."

    - **Maintenance:** "I developed a truly comfortable and satisfying sobriety, but I felt like I was cured. I became complacent and stopped working my recovery program."

5. Enter the Title, Start Date, Stop Date, and Duration for your most recent relapse episode by copying it from your Relapse Episode List.

6. Write a brief description of that relapse episode.

    Example #1: "I started to drink believing I could control it. It worked for awhile, then I lost control and things got as bad as they were."

    Example #2: "I knew I couldn't control it so I didn't try. I just wanted to blot out my pain. The drinking ended up making me feel worse."

7. Describe what you wanted to accomplish by the addictive use.

    Example #1: "I wanted to belong and fit in with my friends who were still drinking and drugging."

    Example #2: "I wanted to stop being so angry and irritable and be able to relax and enjoy life."

    Example #3: "I wanted to have better sex."

8. Did your return to addictive use accomplish for you what you wanted it to accomplish?

9. Copy the severity of consequences from your Relapse Episode List and ask yourself if what you got from your addictive use was worth the price you paid.

9-C
Relapse Episode Analysis

Developed by Terence T. Gorski, 1988

Most Recent Abstinence Period	Start Date	Stop Date	Duration
Title:			

Description: _____

_____

Primary Setups for Relapse: _____

_____

Recovery Stage:	☐ Transition ☐ Middle Recovery	☐ Stabilization ☐ Late Recovery	☐ Early Recovery ☐ Maintenance

Most Recent Relapse Episode	Start Date	Stop Date	Duration
Title:			

Description: _____

_____

What did you want to accomplish with addictive use? _____

_____

Did addictive use give you what you wanted?   ☐ Yes   ☐ No   ☐ Unsure

Severity of Consequences:	☐ Mild	-	Minor Personal Problems
	☐ Moderate	-	Problems to Others, No Serious Damage
	☐ Severe	-	Damage to Others, Health, and Life-style

Second Most Recent Abstinence Period	Start Date	Stop Date	Duration
Title:			

Description: _____

_____

Primary Setups for Relapse: _____

_____

Recovery Stage:
☐ Transition ☐ Stabilization ☐ Early Recovery
☐ Middle Recovery ☐ Late Recovery ☐ Maintenance

Second Most Recent Relapse Episode	Start Date	Stop Date	Duration
Title:			

Description: _____

_____

What did you want to accomplish with addictive use? _____

_____

Did addictive use give you what you wanted? ☐ Yes ☐ No ☐ Unsure

Severity of Consequences:
☐ Mild - Minor Personal Problems
☐ Moderate - Problems to Others, No Serious Damage
☐ Severe - Damage to Others, Health, and Life-style

Third Most Recent Abstinence Period	Start Date	Stop Date	Duration
Title:			

Description: _____

_____

_____

Primary Setups for Relapse: _____

_____

_____

Recovery Stage:
☐ Transition ☐ Stabilization ☐ Early Recovery
☐ Middle Recovery ☐ Late Recovery ☐ Maintenance

Third Most Recent Relapse Episode	Start Date	Stop Date	Duration
Title:			

Description: _____

_____

_____

What did you want to accomplish with addictive use? _____

_____

Did addictive use give you what you wanted?   ☐ Yes   ☐ No   ☐ Unsure

Severity of Consequences:
☐ Mild   - Minor Personal Problems
☐ Moderate - Problems to Others, No Serious Damage
☐ Severe   - Damage to Others, Health, and Life-style

10
The Causes of Relapse

Instructions: There are always causes for relapse. You may not be aware of them, but they are there. Sometimes the causes are internal, something happens inside of you that causes you to start addictive use. At other times the causes are external. You get involved with people or situations that are so stressful or frustrating that it seems like you need to use alcohol or drugs in order to cope.

Until you know what has caused your past relapses you will be condemned to relapse again over the same causes. The following exercises are designed to help you evaluate the causes of your three most recent relapse episodes. You will be asked to think about the internal and external causes of each relapse and then see if you can identify any pattern or sequence of event that led to relapse.

Once you can identify the causes of relapse you can develop strategies for coping with those causes without having to return to addictive use.

10-A
The External Causes of Relapse

Before the most recent relapse episode, I experienced the following:

Problems with Other People: Problems with Situations:

1. _____   1. _____

2. _____   2. _____

3. _____   3. _____

4. _____   4. _____

5. _____   5. _____

Before the second most recent relapse episode, I experienced the following:

Problems with Other People: Problems with Situations:

1. _____   1. _____

2. _____   2. _____

3. _____   3. _____

4. _____   4. _____

5. _____   5. _____

Before the third recent relapse episode, I experienced the following:

Problems with Other People:

1. _____

2. _____

3. _____

4. _____

5. _____

Problems with Situations:

1. _____

2. _____

3. _____

4. _____

5. _____

Factors common to all three episodes:

1. _____

2. _____

3. _____

4. _____

5. _____

6. _____

1. _____

2. _____

3. _____

4. _____

5. _____

6. _____

10-B
The Internal Causes of Relapse

Internal Causes of Relapse: An internal cause of relapse is any problem that you have experienced within yourself that does not involve interaction with other people or direct involvement with situations. The most common internal causes of relapse include both feelings and emotions, and physical pain or illness.

Before the most recent relapse episode, I experienced the following:

Feelings and Emotions:

1. _____

2. _____

3. _____

4. _____

5. _____

Physical Pain or Illness:

1. _____

2. _____

3. _____

4. _____

5. _____

Before the second most recent relapse episode, I experienced the following:

Feelings and Emotions:

1. _____

2. _____

3. _____

4. _____

5. _____

Physical Pain or Illness:

1. _____

2. _____

3. _____

4. _____

5. _____

Before the third recent relapse episode, I experienced the following:

Feelings and Emotions:

1. _____

2. _____

3. _____

4. _____

5. _____

Physical Pain or Illness:

1. _____

2. _____

3. _____

4. _____

5. _____

Factors common to all three episodes:

1. _____

2. _____

3. _____

4. _____

5. _____

6. _____

1. _____

2. _____

3. _____

4. _____

5. _____

6. _____

10-C
The Combined Causes of Relapse

One of the major themes of this workbook is that relapse is always preceded by a sequence of warning signs. With help you can learn to recognize these warning signs and take action to stop them before they begin. To do this you will need to start thinking about the general steps that typically lead up to a relapse. These steps can be thought of as following rules, laws, or principles. If you do certain things it sets you up to relapse. If you do other things, it sets you up to recovery.

Most people find they follow the same steps, with slight variation, before each relapse. This exercise is designed to help you start looking for the pattern that sets you up to relapse. If you can't find it now, don't worry about it. There are more exercises that follow to help you identify and clarify the pattern of setup thoughts and behaviors.

Review the list of external and internal warning signs for all three relapse episodes. See if you can identify a general series of steps that you went through before you began using alcohol or drugs. Write those steps below. If you are not sure, guess at what they might be. Review these forms with your counselor or AA sponsor and tell them the steps to relapse that you discovered. Ask if he / she sees anything that you missed.

The Steps to Alcohol and Drug Use
My First Attempt at Identifying Relapse Warning Signs

Step 1: _____

_____

Step 2: _____

_____

Step 3: _____

_____

Step 4: _____

_____

Step 5: _____

_____

P A R T 2

Warning Sign Identification

E X E R C I S E
11
Relapse Education

Accurate information about relapse and its prevention is essential. The basic knowledge required for a relapse-prone person to achieve long-term sobriety includes knowledge in four areas.

- The Disease of Addiction

- The Recovery Process and How to Develop a Recovery Program

- The Relapse Process

- Relapse Prevention Planning

The first two areas, knowledge about addiction and the recovery process, are reviewed in detail in the book, *Learning to Live again: A Guide to Recovery from Alcoholism*. Knowledge about relapse and relapse prevention planning are reviewed in the book, *Staying Sober: A Guide for Relapse Prevention*. Both of these books are available from Herald House/Independence Press, P.O. Box 390, Independence, MO 64051-0390 (1-800-767-8181).

I strongly recommend that you read both of these books, especially *Staying Sober,* before attempting to complete this manual. The information in these books is an essential preparation for the exercises you will be completing in this workbook. If you have already read these books, it may be helpful to review how much you understand and remember. Immediately following is a self-test which will help you measure your comprehension and understanding of those materials. Following the test is a listing of the correct answers. If you answer any of the questions incorrectly, please turn to the pages indicated and review the information pertaining to that question.

Please take a few moments now to take this test and review the information pertaining to any questions that you answered incorrectly.

11-A
Relapse Education Self-Test

Instructions: The following questions will help you test your understanding about relapse and relapse prevention planning. The numbers at the end of each question refer to the page in *Staying Sober* where you can find that particular information. Read those pages if you do not know the answer to any question or are unsure of any answer.

Part 1: Addictive Disease

1. Addiction is a condition in which a person develops dependence on any mood-altering substance.

   True_____ False _____ (39)

2. The pain of withdrawal is entirely psychological.

   True_____ False _____ (43)

3. High tolerance is an indication that a person is not addicted.

   True_____ False _____ (44)

4. The most effective treatment for alcoholism is Alcoholics Anonymous coupled with professional counseling.

   True_____ False _____ (52)

Part 2: Post Acute Withdrawal

5. Post acute withdrawal occurs before an addicted person goes through the acute abstinence syndrome.

   True_____ False _____ (57)

6. Post acute withdrawal is bio-psycho-social. (58)

   True_____ False _____ (58)

7. Damage to the body and nervous system done by addiction contributes to post acute withdrawal.

   True_____ False _____ (58)

8. Forgetting something you learned 20 minutes before may be a symptom of post acute withdrawal.

   True_____ False _____ (60)

9. Even when sober, a recovering person may experience problems getting the right amount of sleep.

   True_____ False _____ (62)

10. At times of high stress, the symptoms of post acute withdrawal may become worse.

    True_____ False _____ (63)

11. Recovering persons can become unable to recognize and honestly tell others what they are thinking and feeling. (61)

    True_____ False _____

Part 3: Managing Post Acute Withdrawal

12. Poor nutrition and inadequate exercise can create high-risk conditions for a post acute withdrawal episode. (73)

    True_____ False _____

13. Caffeine is a natural stress reducer.

    True_____ False _____ (74, 118)

14. Sweets can prevent symptoms of post acute withdrawal from occurring.

    True_____ False _____ (74)

15. Relaxation exercises can help prevent post acute withdrawal symptoms.

    True_____ False _____ (77, 78)

16. Relaxation exercises cannot reduce already existing post acute withdrawal symptoms.

    True_____ False _____ (77, 78)

17. Laughing and daydreaming are examples of natural stress reducers.

    True_____ False _____ (77)

Part 4: Phases of Recovery

18. Pretreatment is a method to test whether you can control use over a period of time.

    True_____ False _____ (85)

19. Stabilization includes recovery from the severe symptoms of post acute withdrawal.

    True_____ False _____ (87)

20. Early recovery is a time to recover from post acute withdrawal.

    True_____ False _____ (87)

21. Middle recovery is a time to learn how to not use drugs.

    True_____ False _____ (89)

22. Late recovery is a time for personality change.

    True_____ False _____ (90)

23. One task of the maintenance phase of recovery is watching for relapse warning signs.

    True_____ False _____ (93)

24. Partial recovery means you have failed to go to 90 meetings in 90 days.

    True_____ False _____ (93)

Part 5: The Relapse Syndrome

25. Relapse is a process.

    True_____ False _____ (124)

26. There are warning signs that occur long before addictive use begins.

    True_____ False _____ (130)

27. The symptoms of relapse develop subconsciously.

    True_____ False _____ (131)

28. The relapse syndrome usually begins with a breakdown in social structure.

    True_____ False _____ (132)

29. If you have admitted you are an alcoholic, you have overcome denial.

    True_____ False _____ (125)

30. A change in thinking and feeling results in change in behavior.

    True_____ False _____ (132)

Answer Sheet

Part 1: Addictive Disease
1. True
2. False
3. False
4. True

Part 2: Post Acute Withdrawal
5. False
6. True
7. True
8. True
9. True
10. True
11. True

Part 3: Managing Post Acute Withdrawal
12. True
13. False
14. False
15. True
16. True
17. True

Part 4: Phases of Recovery
18. False
19. True
20. False
21. False
22. True
23. True
24. False

Part 5: Relapse Syndrome
25. True
26. True
27. True
28. False
29. False
30. True

12
Relapse Warning Sign Review Sheet

Developed by Terence T. Gorski

The following list of relapse warning signs has been developed to help chemically dependent people recognize the typical sequence of problems that lead them from a comfortable and stable recovery back to chemical use.

Read the list carefully. As you are reading the list:

1. Put a check mark (√) next to any warning sign that you have experienced.

2. Put a question mark (?) next to any warning sign that you have difficulty understanding.

3. Put an asterisk (*) next to any warning sign that causes you to "space out" or to start daydreaming while you are reading it.

Phase I: Internal Change: During this phase I look good on the outside, but I start using old addictive ways of thinking and managing feelings that make me feel bad on the inside. The most common relapse warning signs are:

☐ **1-1. Increased Stress:** I begin to feel more stressed than usual. Sometimes this is the result of a problem or situation that is easy to see. At other times it is the result of little problems that cause stress to build up slowly over time.

☐ **1-2. Change in Thinking:** I begin to think my recovery program is not as important as it used to be. Sometimes things are going so well that I don't believe I need to put a lot of effort into my program. At other times I have problems that my recovery program doesn't seem to help and I ask myself, "why bother?"

☐ **1-3. Change in Feeling:** I start having unpleasant feelings that I don't like. Sometimes I feel euphoric, like everything is going my way when I know that it really is not. At other times I feel depressed, like nothing is working out. I know that these mood sweeps are not good for me.

☐ **1-4. Change in Behavior:** I start acting different. I still look and sound good on the outside, but I know deep inside that I am not practicing my program the way I used to. Deep inside I know something is going wrong.

Phase II: Denial: During this phase, I stop paying attention to or honestly telling others what I am thinking and feeling. The most common relapse warning signs are:

☐ **2-1. Worrying about Myself:** I feel uneasy about the changes in my thinking, feelings, and behavior. This uneasiness comes and goes and usually lasts only a short time. Sometimes I feel afraid that I won't be able to stay sober, but I don't want to think about it.

☐ **2-2. Denying that I'm Worried:** I deal with this uneasiness in the same way I used to deal with my addiction—I go into denial and try to persuade myself that everything is okay when it really isn't. Sometimes the denial works and I can forget my problems and feel better for a little while. I usually don't know that I am using denial when I am doing it. It is only when I think about the situation later that I am able to recognize how bad I was feeling and how I denied those feelings.

PHASE III: Avoidance and Defensiveness: During this phase, I try to avoid anyone or anything that will force me to be honest about how my thinking, feelings, and behavior have changed. If I am confronted directly, I get defensive and can't hear what others are trying to tell me. The most common relapse warning signs are:

☐ **3-1. Believing I'll Never Use Alcohol or Drugs:** I convince myself that I don't need to put a lot of energy into my recovery program today because I will probably never go back to alcohol or drug use. I tend to keep this belief to myself. Sometimes I am afraid to tell my counselor or other recovering people about this belief for fear of being confronted. At other times I think that it is none of their business.

☐ **3-2. Worrying about Others Instead of Self:** I take the focus off myself by becoming more concerned about the sobriety of others than about my personal recovery. I privately judge the drinking or using of my friends and spouse and the recovery programs of other recovering people. I keep these private judgments to myself and don't talk about them. This is often called "working the other guy's program."

☐ **3-3. Defensiveness:** I feel reluctant to discuss personal problems and what I am doing in my recovery because I am afraid I will be criticized or confronted. I feel scared, angry, and defensive when other people ask me questions about my recovery program or point out things about my recovery that I don't want to see. I tend to get defensive even when no defense is necessary.

☐ **3-4. Compulsive Behavior:** I start using compulsive behaviors to keep my mind off how uncomfortable I am feeling. I get stuck in old, rigid, and self-defeating ways of thinking and acting. I tend to do the same things over and over again without a good reason. I try to control conversations either by talking too much or not talking at all. I start working more than I need to and get involved in many activities. Other people think I am the model of recovery because of my heavy involvement in Twelve-Step work and chairing meetings. I become active in my therapy group by "playing therapist" but I am reluctant to talk about my personal problems. I avoid casual or informal involvement with people unless I can be in control.

☐ **3-5. Impulsive Behavior:** I start creating problems for myself by using poor judgment and impulsively doing things without thinking them through. This usually happens at times of high stress. Sometimes I privately feel bad, but I tend to make excuses and blame others for the problems.

☐ **3-6. Tendencies toward Loneliness:** I start feeling uncomfortable around others and start spending more time alone. I usually have good reasons and excuses for staying away from other people. I start feeling lonely. Instead of dealing with the loneliness by trying to meet and be around other people, I get more compulsive about doing things alone.

PHASE IV: Crisis Building: During this phase, I start having problems in sobriety that I don't understand. Even though I want to solve these problems and work hard at it, two new problems pop up to replace every problem that I solve. The most common warning signs are:

☐ **4-1. Tunnel Vision:** I start to think my life is made up of separate and unrelated parts. I focus on one small part of my life and block out everything else. Sometimes I focus only on the good things and block out or ignore the bad. In this way I can mistakenly believe everything is fine when it really isn't. At other times I see only what is going wrong and blow that out of proportion. This causes me to feel like nothing is going my way even when there are many good things happening in my life. As a result I can't see "the big picture" or figure out how what I do in one part of my life can cause problems in other parts of my life. When problems develop I don't know why. I believe that life is unfair and that I have no power to do anything about it.

☐ **4-2. Minor Depression:** I start to feel depressed, down, blue, listless, and empty of feelings. I lack energy, tend to sleep too much, and rarely feel good or full of life. I am able to distract myself from these moods by getting busy with other things and not talking about the depression.

☐ 4-3. **Loss of Constructive Planning:** I stop planning ahead and thinking about what I am going to do next. I begin to think that the slogan, "One Day at a Time," means that I should not plan ahead or think about what I am going to do. I pay less and less attention to details. I become listless. My plans are based more on wishful thinking (how I wish things would be) than reality (how things actually are). As a result I make plans that are not realistic and stop paying attention to the details of implementing those plans.

☐ 4-4. **Plans Begin to Fail:** My plans begin to fail and each failure causes new problems. I tend to overreact to or mismanage each problem in a way that creates a new and bigger problem. I start having the same kind of problems with work, friends, family, and money that I used to have when I was using addictively. I feel guilty and remorseful when I have these problems. I work hard trying to solve them, but something always seems to go wrong that creates an even bigger or more depressing problem.

PHASE V: Immobilization: During this phase, I feel trapped in an endless stream of unmanageable problems and feel like giving up. I can't seem to get started or make myself do the things that I know I need to do.

☐ 5-1. **Daydreaming and Wishful Thinking:** It becomes more difficult to concentrate or figure things out. I have fantasies of escaping or "being rescued from it all" by an event unlikely to happen. The "if only" syndrome becomes more common in conversation. I start daydreaming and wishing for things that I want without doing anything to try to get them.

☐ 5-2. **Feelings that Nothing Can Be Solved:** I begin to feel like a failure who will never be able to get anything right. The failures may be real or imagined. I exaggerate small problems and blow them out of proportion while failing to notice anything that I do right. I start to believe that "I've tried my best and recovery isn't working out."

☐ 5-3. **Immature Wish to Be Happy:** I have a vague desire "to be happy" or to have "things work out," but I don't set up any plans to make those things happen. I want to be happy but I have no idea what I can do to make myself happy. I am not willing to work hard or pay the price for the happiness that I want. I start wishing that something magical would happen to rescue me from my problems.

PHASE VI: Confusion and Overreaction: During this phase I have trouble thinking clearly and managing my thoughts, feelings, and actions. I am irritable and tend to overreact to small things. The most common relapse warning signs are:

☐ 6-1. **Difficulty in Thinking Clearly:** I start to have trouble thinking clearly and solving usually simple problems. Sometimes my mind races and I can't shut it off while at other times it seems to shut off or go blank. My mind tends to wander and I have difficulty thinking about something for more than a few minutes. I get confused and have trouble figuring out how one thing relates to or affects other things. I also have difficulty deciding what to do next in order to manage my life and recovery. As a result I tend to make bad decisions that I would not have made if I were thinking clearly.

☐ 6-2. **Difficulty in Managing Feelings and Emotions:** I start to have difficulty managing my feelings and emotions. Sometimes I overreact emotionally and feel too much. At other times I become emotionally numb and can't figure out what I am feeling. Sometimes I feel strange or have "crazy feelings" for no apparent reason. I start to think that I might be going crazy. I have strong mood swings and periodically feel depressed, anxious, and scared. As a result, I don't trust my feelings and emotions and often try to ignore, stuff, or forget about them. My mood sweeps start causing me new problems.

☐ 6-3. **Difficulty in Remembering Things:** At times I have problems remembering things and learning new information and skills. Things I want to remember seem to dissolve or evaporate from my mind within minutes. I also have problems remembering key events from my childhood, adolescence, or adulthood. At times I remember things clearly, but at other times these same memories will not come to mind. I feel blocked, stuck, or cut off from these memories. At times, the inability to remember things causes me to make bad decisions that I would not have made if my memory were working properly.

☐ 6-4. **Periods of Confusion:** I start getting confused more often, and the confusion is more severe and lasts longer. I'm not sure what is right or wrong. I don't know what to do to solve my problems because everything I try seems to make them worse. I get angry at myself because I can't solve my problems and just keep making things worse.

☐ 6-5. **Difficulty in Managing Stress:** I start having trouble dealing with stress. Sometimes I feel numb and can't recognize the minor signs of daily stress. At other times I seem overwhelmed by severe stress for no real reason. When I feel stressed out I cannot relax no matter what I do. The things other people do to relax either don't work for me or they make the stress worse. It seems I get so tense that I am not in control. The stress starts to get so bad that I can't do the things I normally do. I get afraid that I will collapse physically or emotionally.

☐ 6-6. **Irritation with Friends:** My relationships with friends, family, counselors, and other recovering people became strained. Sometimes I feel threatened when others talk about the changes they are noticing in my behavior and moods. At other times I just don't care about what they say. The arguments and conflicts get worse despite my efforts to resolve them. I start to feel guilty.

☐ 6-7. **Easily Angered:** I feel irritable and frustrated. I start losing my temper for no real reason and feeling guilty afterward. I often overreact to small things that really shouldn't make any difference. I start avoiding people because I am afraid I might lose control and get violent. The effort to control myself adds to the stress and tension.

PHASE VII: Depression: During this phase I become so depressed that I can't do the things I normally do. At times I feel life is not worth living, and sometimes I think about killing myself or using alcohol or other drugs as a way to end the depression. I am so depressed that I can't hide it from others. The most common relapse warning signs are:

☐ 7-1. **Irregular Eating Habits:** I either start to overeat or I lose my appetite and eat very little. As a result I start gaining or losing weight. I skip meals and stop eating at regular times. I replace a well-balanced, nourishing diet with "junk food."

☐ 7-2. **Lack of Desire to Take Action:** I can't get started or get anything done. At those times I am unable to concentrate, feel anxious, fearful, uneasy, and often feel trapped with no way out.

☐ 7-3. **Difficulty Sleeping Restfully:** I cannot fall asleep. When I do sleep, I have unusual or disturbing dreams, awaken many times, and have difficulty falling back to sleep. I sleep fitfully and rarely experience a deep, relaxing sleep. I awaken from a night of sleep feeling tired. The times of day during which I sleep change. At times I stay up late due to an inability to fall asleep and then oversleep because I am too tired to get up in the morning. At other times I become so exhausted that I sleep for extremely long periods, sometimes sleeping around the clock for one or more days.

☐ 7-4. **Loss of Daily Structure:** My daily routine becomes haphazard. I stop getting up and going to bed at regular times. I start skipping meals and eating at unusual times. I find it hard to keep appointments and plan social events. I feel rushed and overburdened at times and then have nothing to do at other times. I am unable to follow through on plans and decisions and experience tension, frustration, fear, or anxiety which keeps me from doing what I know needs to be done.

☐ 7-5. **Periods of Deep Depression:** I feel depressed more often. The depression becomes worse, lasts longer, and interferes with living. The depression is so bad it is noticed by others and cannot be easily denied. The depression is most severe during unplanned or unstructured periods of time. Fatigue, hunger, and loneliness make the depression worse. When I feel depressed, I separate from other people, become irritable and angry with others, and often complain that nobody cares or understands what I am going through.

PHASE VIII: Behavioral Loss of Control: During this phase I can't control my thoughts, feelings, and behavior. I can't stick to a productive daily schedule. I am still denying how dysfunctional I have become, and I am not willing to admit that I am out of control even though my life is chaotic and I have serious problems. The most common warning signs are:

☐ 8-1. **Irregular Attendance at AA and Treatment Meetings:** I start finding excuses to miss therapy and self-help group meetings. I find excuses to justify this and don't recognize the importance of AA and treatment. I develop the attitude that "AA and counseling aren't making me feel better, so why should I make them a number-one priority? Other things are more important."

☐ 8-2. **An "I Don't Care" Attitude:** I try to act as if I don't care about the problems that are occurring. This is to hide feelings of helplessness and a growing lack of self-respect and self-confidence.

☐ 8-3. **Open Rejection of Help:** I cut myself off from people who can help. I may do this by having fits of anger that drive others away, by criticizing and putting others down, or by quietly withdrawing from others.

☐ 8-4. **Dissatisfaction with Life:** Things seem so bad that I begin to think I might as well go back to alcohol or drug use because things couldn't get worse. Life seems to have become unmanageable even though I am sober and not using addictively.

☐ 8-5. **Feelings of Powerlessness and Helplessness:** I have trouble "getting started." I have difficulty thinking clearly, concentrating, and thinking abstractly. I feel that I can't do anything and begin to believe there is no way out.

PHASE IX: Recognition of Loss of Control: During this phase my denial breaks and I suddenly recognize how severe my problems are, how unmanageable life has become, and how little power and control I have to solve any of the problems. This awareness is very painful and frightening. By this time I have become so isolated that it seems that there is no one to turn to for help. The most common warning signs are:

☐ 9-1. **Difficulty with Physical Coordination and Accidents:** I start having difficulty with physical coordination that results in dizziness, poor balance, difficulty with hand-eye coordination, or slow reflexes. These problems cause me to feel clumsy and become accident prone.

☐ 9-2. **Self-pity:** I begin to feel sorry for myself and may use self-pity to get attention at AA or from family members. I feel ashamed because I think I must be crazy, emotionally disturbed, defective as a person, or incapable of being or feeling normal. I also feel guilty because I believe I am doing things wrong or failing to work a proper recovery program. The shame and guilt cause me to hide the warning signs and stop talking honestly with others about what I am experiencing. The longer I keep the warning signs hidden, the stronger they become. I try to manage the warning signs and find that I can't do it. As a result I begin to believe that I must be hopeless and I feel sorry for myself.

☐ 9-3. **Thoughts of Social Use:** I start to think that alcohol or drug use will help me feel better. I start hoping that I can one day return to social drinking and recreational drug use. I think I might really be able to control it next time. Sometimes I am able to put these thoughts out of my mind, but often the thoughts are so strong that they cannot be stopped. I may begin to feel that alcohol or drug use is the only alternative to going crazy or committing suicide. Using alcohol and drugs actually looks like a sane and rational alternative.

☐ **9-4. Conscious Lying:** I know that I am lying, using denial and making excuses for my behavior, but I can't stop myself. I feel out of control. I start doing things on a regular basis that I normally would not do that violate my values. I just can't seem to stop myself or control my behavior.

☐ **9-5. Complete Loss of Self-confidence:** I feel trapped and overwhelmed because I can't think clearly or do the things I know I need to do to solve my problems. I feel powerless and hopeless. I start to believe that I am useless, incompetent, and will never be able to manage my life.

Phase X: Option Reduction: During this phase I feel trapped by the pain and inability to manage my life. I start to believe that there are only three ways out — insanity, suicide, or self-medication with alcohol or drugs. I no longer believe anyone or anything can help me. The most common warning signs that occur during this phase are:

☐ **10-1. Unreasonable Resentment:** I feel angry because of the inability to behave the way I want to. Sometimes the anger is with the world in general, sometimes with someone or something in particular, and sometimes with myself.

☐ **10-2. Discontinues All Treatment and AA:** I stop attending all AA meetings. If I am taking Antabuse, I may forget to take it or deliberately avoid taking it regularly. If a sponsor or helping person is part of treatment, tension and conflict develop and become so severe that the relationship usually ends. I may drop out of professional counseling even though I need help and know it.

☐ **10-3. Overwhelming Loneliness, Frustration, Anger, and Tension:** I feel completely overwhelmed. I believe there is no way out except drinking, suicide, or insanity. I feel like I am helpless, desperate, and about to go crazy.

☐ **10-4. Loss of Behavioral Control:** I experience more and more difficulty in controlling thoughts, emotions, judgments, and behaviors. This progressive and disabling loss of control begins to cause serious problems in all areas of life, including my health. No matter how hard I try to regain control, I am unable to do so.

PHASE XI: Alcohol and Drug Use: During this phase I return to alcohol or drug use, try to control it, lose control, and realize that my addiction is once again destroying my life.

☐ **11-1. Attempting Controlled Use:** I convince myself that I have no choice but to use alcohol or drugs and that using will somehow make my problems better or allow me to escape from them for a little while. I plan to try either social use or a short-term binge. If I try to be a controlled social or recreational user, I start using a little bit on a regular basis. If I decide to go out on a short-term binge, I plan a chemical-use episode that will be a "one-time only, time-limited, controlled binge."

☐ **11-2. Disappointment, Shame, and Guilt:** I feel disappointed because alcohol and drugs don't do for me what I thought they would. I feel guilty because I believe I have done something wrong by using addictively. I feel ashamed because I start to believe I am defective and worthless as a person, and my relapse proves it."

☐ **11-3. Loss of Control:** My alcohol or drug use spirals out of control. Sometimes I lose control slowly. At other times, the loss of control is very rapid. I begin using as often and as much as before.

☐ **11-4. Life and Health Problems:** I start having severe problems with my life and health. Marriage, jobs, and friendships are seriously damaged. Eventually, my physical health suffers and I become so ill that I need professional treatment.

Appendix: Developmental History of the Relapse Warning Sign List

Terence T. Gorski began working with relapse-prone chemically dependent patients in the early 1970s.

Relapse is a process that begins long before chemically dependent people begin to use alcohol or other drugs. The relapse process begins when chemically dependent people begin mismanaging problems in sobriety and, as a result, feel progressive pain and discomfort in sobriety. This pain and discomfort can become so severe that they cannot live normally in recovery. In AA this is called a "dry drunk." Other people call it building up to drink (BUD). Recovering people can start hurting so bad they convince themselves that chemical use can't be any worse than the pain of staying sober.

The first Relapse Warning Sign List was developed by Terence T. Gorski in 1973 after he completed and analyzed the relapse histories of 118 relapse-prone alcoholic patients. These alcoholics had four things in common: (1) they had completed a 21- or 28-day rehabilitation program for alcoholism; (2) they had recognized they were alcoholic and could not safely use alcohol or other drugs; (3) when they left rehabilitation they had the conscious intention of staying permanently sober by using both Alcoholics Anonymous (AA) and professional counseling; and, (4) they eventually returned to the addictive use of alcohol or drugs despite their initial commitment to remain sober.

The most common reported symptoms in this clinical research were compiled into a relapse chart containing 37 relapse warning signs. This chart was given to patients during a lecture about relapse warning signs. They were asked to circle the warning signs that they identified with on the chart and discuss them later in group therapy.

In 1975 Terence Gorski developed a pamphlet that contained brief descriptions of each of the 37 warning signs that appeared on the Warning Sign Chart. In 1977 this pamphlet was updated by dividing the 37 warning signs into ten phases to make them easier to understand and remember. Merlene Miller edited this list to make it easier to read and use with patients.

The Relapse Warning Signs were first published in *The EAP Digest* (November/December 1980). They were next published in the book, *Learning to Live Again* by Merlene Miller and Terence T. Gorski, in 1982. The warning signs were revised again when *The Staying Sober Workbook* was published in 1988. This revision added information about post acute withdrawal (PAW) as phase one of the process, thus expanding the warning sign progression to include eleven rather than the original ten phases.

In 1993 the Relapse Warning Sign List was revised again to simplify the language further and provide a better integration of the PAW symptoms into the progression of warning sign severity.

E X E R C I S E
13
The Initial Warning Sign List

Instructions: The Initial Warning Sign List is designed to help you select and personalize three warning signs from the composite list with which you identify.

1. Review the composite list of relapse warning signs and select three warning signs with which you identify.

2. Enter the title of the first warning sign you selected on the initial warning sign list in the space labeled "Original Title. (A)

3. Answer the question, "Why did I select the warning sign?" in the indicated place. (B)

4. Read the first warning sign that you selected again and underline the most important word or phrase in the description. Write that word or phrase in the space labeled "Underlined Word or Phrase." (C)

5. Describe what that word or phrase means to you in the indicated space. (D)

6. Give this warning sign a new title by describing it in words that feel right to you and will be easy for you to remember in the space labeled "Personalized Title." (E)

7. Write a new description of the warning sign in your own words starting with the phrase, "I know I am in trouble with my recovery when ...".

8. Repeat steps two to seven for the other two warning signs that you selected.

9. Write the thoughts that popped into your head while you were completing the Initial Warning Sign List after Item 4.

10. Identify any feelings you experienced while completing the Initial Warning Sign List after Item 5.

11. Complete the sentence "I am now becoming aware that ..." ten times as fast as you can with different answers after Item 6.

12. Identify any hidden warning signs that you became aware of while completing the Initial Warning Sign List.

The Initial Warning Sign List

Developed by Terence T. Gorski, 1985

1. **The First Warning Sign:**

   (A) Original title: _____

   (B) Why I selected this warning sign: _____

   _____

   (C) Underlined word or phrase: _____

   (D) What this word or phrase means to me is ...

   _____

   _____

   (E) Personalized title: _____

   (F) Personalized description: I know I am in trouble with my recovery when ....

   _____

   _____

   _____

2. **The Second Warning Sign:**

   (A) Original Title: _____

   (B) Why I selected this warning sign: _____

   _____

   (C) Underlined word or phrase: _____

(D) What this word or phrase means to me is...

_____

_____

(E) Personalized title: _____

(F) Personalized description: I know I am in trouble with my recovery when ...

_____

_____

3. **The Third Warning Sign:**

(A) Original title: _____

(B) Why I selected this warning sign: _____

_____

_____

(C) Underlined word or phrase: _____

(D) What this word or phrase means to me is ...

_____

_____

(E) Personalized title: _____

(F) Personalized description: I know I am in trouble with my recovery when ...

_____

_____

_____

4. **Automatic Thoughts:** What thoughts popped into your head as you were completing this worksheet?

_____

_____

_____

_____

_____

5. **Automatic Feelings:** What feelings did you experience while you were completing this worksheet?

_____

_____

_____

6. **Sentence Completion:** Please complete the following sentence as fast as you can with ten different endings: "I am now becoming aware that ..."

(1) _____

(2) _____

(3) _____

(4) _____

(5) _____

(6) _____

(7) _____

(8) _____

(9) _____

(10) _____

7. **Hidden Warning Signs:** While completing this worksheet, did you think of any other warning signs or problems related to your past relapses?

_____

_____

_____

_____

_____

_____

_____

_____

_____

14
Introduction to Warning Sign Analysis

Developed by Terence T. Gorski, 1985

Most people who relapse believe they know what causes them to return to alcohol and drug use. When they carefully examine the events that lead to relapse, they often find that there are many hidden causes of relapse. I call these hidden causes "hidden warning signs."

The purpose of the next exercise is to help you think through in detail past events which caused relapse. I also will ask you to use your imagination and think about things that could cause you to return to addictive use in the future.

The process is rather long and detailed, but I encourage you to be as patient as you can and complete the whole process. The more hidden warning signs that you are able to uncover as a result of this process, the more likely it is that you will be able to identify and manage them before you return to addictive use.

14-A
Warning Sign Analysis #1

Developed by Terence T. Gorski, 1985

Instructions: Analyze the first warning sign on your Initial Warning Sign List using this procedure:

1. **Select the First Warning Sign:** What is the first warning sign from your initial warning sign list that you would like to learn more about?

   _____

2. **Description:** How do you know when you are experiencing this warning sign?

   _____

   _____

   _____

   _____

   A. **Thinking:** What are you usually thinking when you experience this warning sign?

   _____

   _____

   _____

   B. **Feeling:** What are you usually feeling when you experience this warning sign?

   _____

   _____

   _____

C. **Action:** What do you have an urge to do when you experience this warning sign? What do you actually do?

_____

_____

_____

_____

_____

3. **Hidden Warning Signs:** Read what you have written and look for hidden warning signs that are part of the description. Write these new hidden warning signs in complete sentences in your own words on your Warning Sign Identification Cards.

- Use one card for each new hidden warning sign.

- Write a brief title for each.

- Write a one sentence description for each key idea that begins with the words, "I know I am in trouble with my recovery when ...".

- Take a deep breath and read the sentence out loud to yourself several times to make sure it feels right to you. If it doesn't feel right when you read it out loud, write it again using different words.

4. **Arrange the Cards in Order:** Arrange your cards in the order in which the warning signs generally occur. Eliminate obvious duplications.

5. **Past Experience:** Please describe a specific past experience when you experienced this warning sign while sober.

A. The warning sign was triggered when _____

_____

_____

_____

_____

_____

B. The first thing I did was _____

_____

_____

_____

_____

C. The next thing I did was _____

_____

_____

_____

_____

D. What finally happened was _____

_____

_____

_____

_____

E. Where did this happen? _____

_____

_____

_____

_____

F. When did this happen? (Time of year? Day of the week? Time of the day?)

_____

_____

_____

G. What were you doing when the warning sign was triggered?

_____

_____

_____

H. Who were you with and what were they doing?

_____

_____

_____

I. What was going on around you?

_____

_____

_____

J. What did you feel an urge to do?

_____

_____

_____

K. What did you actually do?

_____

_____

_____

_____

_____

6. **Hidden Warning Signs:** Read what you have written and look for hidden warning signs that are part of the description. Write these new hidden warning signs in complete sentences in your own words on your Warning Sign Identification Cards.

   - Use one card for each new hidden warning sign.

   - Write a brief title for each.

   - Write a one sentence description for each key idea that begins with the words "I know I am in trouble with my recovery when ...".

   - Take a deep breath and read the sentence out loud to yourself several times to make sure it feels right to you. If it doesn't feel right when you read it out loud, write it again using different words.

7. **Arrange the Cards in Order:** Add the new cards to the previous cards. Be sure to arrange the cards in the correct sequence and to eliminate obvious duplications.

8. **Future Experience:** Please describe a specific future experience when you believe you will experience this warning sign while sober.

   A. This warning sign will probably get triggered in the future when....

_____

_____

_____

_____

_____

B. The first thing I will do is _____

_____

_____

_____

_____

C. The next thing I will do is_____

_____

_____

_____

_____

D. What will finally happen is_____

_____

_____

_____

_____

E. Where will you probably be when this happens? _____

_____

_____

_____

_____

F. When is this most likely to happen? (Time of year? Day of the week? Time of the day?)

_____

_____

_____

_____

G. What are you most likely to be doing when the warning sign gets triggered?

_____

_____

_____

_____

H. Who are you most likely to be with and what are they going to be doing?

_____

_____

_____

_____

I. What will be going on around you?

_____

_____

_____

_____

J. What will you probably feel an urge to do?

_____

_____

_____

K.   What will you actually do?

_____

_____

_____

_____

_____

9.   **Hidden Warning Signs:** Read what you have written and look for hidden warning signs that are part of the description. Write these new hidden warning signs in complete sentences in your own words on your Warning Sign Identification Cards.

   • Use one card for each new hidden warning sign.

   • Write a brief title for each.

   • Write a one sentence description for each key idea that begins with the words, "I know I am in trouble with my recovery when ...".

   • Take a deep breath and read the sentence out loud to yourself several times to make sure it feels right to you. If it doesn't feel right when you read it out loud, write it again using different words.

10. **Arrange the Cards in Order:** Arrange your cards in the order in which the warning signs generally occur. Eliminate obvious duplications.

14-B
Warning Sign Analysis #2

Developed by Terence T. Gorski, 1985

Instructions: Analyze the second warning sign on your Initial Warning Sign List using this procedure:

1. **Select the Second Warning Sign:** What is the first warning sign from your initial warning sign list that you would like to learn more about?

   _____

2. **Description:** How do you know when you are experiencing this warning sign?

   _____

   _____

   _____

   _____

   A. **Thinking:** What are you usually thinking when you experience this warning sign?

   _____

   _____

   _____

   _____

   B. **Feeling:** What are you usually feeling when you experience this warning sign?

   _____

   _____

   _____

   _____

C. **Action:** What do you have an urge to do when you experience this warning sign? What do you actually do?

_____

_____

_____

_____

3. **Hidden Warning Signs:** Read what you have written and look for hidden warning signs that are part of the description. Write these new hidden warning signs in complete sentences in your own words on your Warning Sign Identification Cards.

   - Use one card for each new hidden warning sign.

   - Write a brief title for each.

   - Write a one sentence description for each key idea that begins with the words, "I know I am in trouble with my recovery when ...".

   - Take a deep breath and read the sentence out loud to yourself several times to make sure it feels right to you. If it doesn't feel right when you read it out loud, write it again using different words.

4. **Arrange the Cards in Order:** Arrange your cards in the order in which the warning signs generally occur. Eliminate obvious duplications.

5. **Past Experience:** Please describe a specific past experience when you experienced this warning sign while sober.

   A. The warning sign was triggered when _____

_____

_____

_____

_____

_____

B. The first thing I did was _____

_____

_____

_____

_____

C. The next thing I did was _____

_____

_____

_____

_____

D. What finally happened was _____

_____

_____

_____

_____

E. Where did this happen? _____

_____

_____

_____

_____

F. When did this happen? (Time of year? Day of the week? Time of the day?)

_____

_____

_____

_____

G. What were you doing when the warning sign was triggered?

_____

_____

_____

_____

H. Who were you with and what were they doing?

_____

_____

_____

_____

I. What was going on around you?

_____

_____

_____

_____

J. What did you feel an urge to do?

_____

_____

_____

K. What did you actually do?

_____

_____

_____

_____

_____

6. **Hidden Warning Signs:** Read what you have written and look for hidden warning signs that are part of the description. Write these new hidden warning signs in complete sentences in your own words on your Warning Sign Identification Cards.

- Use one card for each new hidden warning sign.

- Write a brief title for each.

- Write a one sentence description for each key idea that begins with the words "I know I am in trouble with my recovery when ...".

- Take a deep breath and read the sentence out loud to yourself several times to make sure it feels right to you. If it doesn't feel right when you read it out loud, write it again using different words.

7. **Arrange the Cards in Order:** Add the new cards to the previous cards. Be sure to arrange the cards in the correct sequence and to eliminate obvious duplications.

8. **Future Experience:** Please describe a specific future experience when you believe you will experience this warning sign while sober.

A. This warning sign will probably get triggered in the future when....

_____

_____

_____

_____

_____

B.   The first thing I will do is _____

_____

_____

_____

_____

C.   The next thing I will do is_____

_____

_____

_____

_____

D.   What will finally happen is_____

_____

_____

_____

_____

E.   Where will you probably be when this happens? _____

_____

_____

_____

_____

F. When is this most likely to happen? (Time of year? Day of the week? Time of the day?)

_____

_____

_____

_____

G. What are you most likely to be doing when the warning sign gets triggered?

_____

_____

_____

_____

H. Who are you most likely to be with and what are they going to be doing?

_____

_____

_____

_____

I. What will be going on around you?

_____

_____

_____

_____

J. What will you probably feel an urge to do?

_____

_____

_____

K.   What will you actually do?

_____

_____

_____

_____

_____

9.   **Hidden Warning Signs:** Read what you have written and look for hidden warning signs that are part of the description. Write these new hidden warning signs in complete sentences in your own words on your Warning Sign Identification Cards.

   • Use one card for each new hidden warning sign.

   • Write a brief title for each.

   • Write a one sentence description for each key idea that begins with the words, "I know I am in trouble with my recovery when ...".

   • Take a deep breath and read the sentence out loud to yourself several times to make sure it feels right to you. If it doesn't feel right when you read it out loud, write it again using different words.

10. **Arrange the Cards in Order:** Arrange your cards in the order in which the warning signs generally occur. Eliminate obvious duplications.

14-C
Warning Sign Analysis #3

Developed by Terence T. Gorski, 1985

Instructions: Analyze the third warning sign on your Initial Warning Sign List using this procedure:

1. **Select the Third Warning Sign:** What is the first warning sign from your initial warning sign list that you would like to learn more about?

   _____

2. **Description:** How do you know when you are experiencing this warning sign?

   _____

   _____

   _____

   _____

   A. **Thinking:** What are you usually thinking when you experience this warning sign?

   _____

   _____

   _____

   _____

   B. **Feeling:** What are you usually feeling when you experience this warning sign?

   _____

   _____

   _____

   _____

C. **Action:** What do you have an urge to do when you experience this warning sign? What do you actually do?

_____

_____

_____

_____

_____

3. **Hidden Warning Signs:** Read what you have written and look for hidden warning signs that are part of the description. Write these new hidden warning signs in complete sentences in your own words on your Warning Sign Identification Cards.

- Use one card for each new hidden warning sign.

- Write a brief title for each.

- Write a one sentence description for each key idea that begins with the words, "I know I am in trouble with my recovery when ...".

- Take a deep breath and read the sentence out loud to yourself several times to make sure it feels right to you. If it doesn't feel right when you read it out loud, write it again using different words.

4. **Arrange the Cards in Order:** Arrange your cards in the order in which the warning signs generally occur. Eliminate obvious duplications.

5. **Past Experience:** Please describe a specific past experience when you experienced this warning sign while sober.

A. The warning sign was triggered when _____

_____

_____

_____

_____

_____

131

B. The first thing I did was _____

_____

_____

_____

_____

C. The next thing I did was _____

_____

_____

_____

_____

D. What finally happened was _____

_____

_____

_____

_____

E. Where did this happen? _____

_____

_____

_____

_____

F. When did this happen? (Time of year? Day of the week? Time of the day?)

_____

_____

_____

G. What were you doing when the warning sign was triggered?

_____

_____

_____

H. Who were you with and what were they doing?

_____

_____

_____

I. What was going on around you?

_____

_____

_____

J. What did you feel an urge to do?

_____

_____

_____

K. What did you actually do?

_____

_____

_____

_____

_____

6. **Hidden Warning Signs:** Read what you have written and look for hidden warning signs that are part of the description. Write these new hidden warning signs in complete sentences in your own words on your Warning Sign Identification Cards.

    - Use one card for each new hidden warning sign.

    - Write a brief title for each.

    - Write a one sentence description for each key idea that begins with the words "I know I am in trouble with my recovery when ...".

    - Take a deep breath and read the sentence out loud to yourself several times to make sure it feels right to you. If it doesn't feel right when you read it out loud, write it again using different words.

7. **Arrange the Cards in Order:** Add the new cards to the previous cards. Be sure to arrange the cards in the correct sequence and to eliminate obvious duplications.

8. **Future Experience:** Please describe a specific future experience when you believe you will experience this warning sign while sober.

    A. This warning sign will probably get triggered in the future when....

    _____

    _____

    _____

    _____

    _____

B.   The first thing I will do is _____

_____

_____

_____

_____

C.   The next thing I will do is _____

_____

_____

_____

_____

D.   What will finally happen is _____

_____

_____

_____

_____

E.   Where will you probably be when this happens? _____

_____

_____

_____

_____

F. When is this most likely to happen? (Time of year? Day of the week? Time of the day?)

_____

_____

_____

_____

G. What are you most likely to be doing when the warning sign gets triggered?

_____

_____

_____

_____

H. Who are you most likely to be with and what are they going to be doing?

_____

_____

_____

_____

I. What will be going on around you?

_____

_____

_____

_____

J. What will you probably feel an urge to do?

_____

_____

_____

K. What will you actually do?

_____

_____

_____

_____

_____

9. **Hidden Warning Signs:** Read what you have written and look for hidden warning signs that are part of the description. Write these new hidden warning signs in complete sentences in your own words on your Warning Sign Identification Cards.

    - Use one card for each new hidden warning sign.

    - Write a brief title for each.

    - Write a one sentence description for each key idea that begins with the words, "I know I am in trouble with my recovery when ...".

    - Take a deep breath and read the sentence out loud to yourself several times to make sure it feels right to you. If it doesn't feel right when you read it out loud, write it again using different words.

10. **Arrange the Cards in Order:** Arrange your cards in the order in which the warning signs generally occur. Eliminate obvious duplications.

14-D
Reactions to Warning Sign Analysis

1. **Read Your Warning Sign Cards:** Read your warning signs cards out loud in the correct order. If possible, read them to another person and explain the story of how you progress from stable recovery to addictive use. As you read the cards out loud, notice the thoughts that pop into your head, the feelings they stir up, and what you have an urge to do.

    A. **Thoughts:** What thoughts popped into your head while reading the cards?

    _____

    _____

    _____

    _____

    B. **Feelings:** What feelings did you experience while reading the warning sign cards?

    _____

    _____

    _____

    _____

    C. **Action Urges:** What did you have an urge to do to deal with the thoughts and feelings?

    _____

    _____

    _____

    _____

E X E R C I S E
15
Sentence Completion

Instructions: In this exercise you will use a technique called sentence completion to help identify hidden warning signs that have been repressed or blocked from conscious awareness.

1. **Centering Technique:** Take a deep breath, hold it and slowly exhale. Relax and notice how your stomach, chest, and throat feel. Take a final deep breath, exhale, and notice how you are feeling.

2. **Read Your Warning Sign Cards:** Read the front side of your warning sign identification cards and notice how you are feeling as you read each warning sign.

Sentence Completion #1

Instructions: Complete the following sentence stem with a different answer at least ten times. There are no right or wrong answers and it is okay to write things that are unusual, silly, or don't make sense. Relax and let yourself write whatever pops into your mind. Ignore the yes or no answers at the end of each line. You will complete those answers in the next part of the exercise.

"I know I am in trouble with my recovery when..."   Is this a
                                                                      hot response?

1. _____ ☐ Yes ☐ No

   _____

2. _____ ☐ Yes ☐ No

   _____

3. _____ ☐ Yes ☐ No

   _____

4. _____ ☐ Yes ☐ No

   _____

5. _____ ☐ Yes ☐ No

   _____

6. _____ ☐ Yes ☐ No

   _____

7. _____ ☐ Yes ☐ No

   _____

8. _____ ☐ Yes ☐ No

   _____

9. _____ ☐ Yes ☐ No

   _____

10. _____ ☐ Yes ☐ No

   _____

Hot Responses

Instructions: A hot response is any answer to a sentence completion that causes you to remember an unpleasant memory, have a strong feeling, or start a private argument within yourself.

1. Read the list of answers that you have just written.

2. As you read each answer, take a deep breath and notice what you are thinking and feeling.

3. Decide if that answer is a hot response (i.e., does it stir up an unpleasant memory, cause a strong feeling, or cause you to start an argument within yourself?).

4. At the end of each answer is the question, "Is this a hot response?" followed by a place to answer "yes" or "no." Check "yes" if the statement is a hot response. Check "no" if the statement is not a hot response.

Writing the First New Sentence Stem

Select one hot response that you would like to work with and write a new sentence stem using that response. The following examples will show you how to create a new sentence stem from a hot response.

If the hot response is...	**The new sentence stem will be...**
I know I am in trouble with my recovery when I argue with my wife.	I argue with my wife when ...
I know I am in trouble with my recovery when I feel angry for no reason.	I feel angry for no reason when ...
I know I am in trouble with my recovery when I start to work long hours.	I work long hours when...

1. The hot response I want to work with is...

_____

2. The new sentence stem is ...

_____

Sentence Completion #2

Instructions: Write your new sentence stem in the space below:

_____

Complete that sentence stem with a different answer at least ten times. Ignore the yes or no answers at the end of each line. You will complete those answers in the next part of the exercise.

Is this a
hot response?

1. _____ ☐ Yes ☐ No

   _____

2. _____ ☐ Yes ☐ No

   _____

3. _____ ☐ Yes ☐ No

   _____

4. _____ ☐ Yes ☐ No

   _____

5. _____ ☐ Yes ☐ No

   _____

6. _____ ☐ Yes ☐ No

   _____

7. _____ ☐ Yes ☐ No

   _____

8. _____ ☐ Yes ☐ No

   _____

9. _____ ☐ Yes ☐ No

   _____

10. _____ ☐ Yes ☐ No

    _____

Hot Responses

Instructions:

1. Read the list of answers that you have just written.

2. As you read each answer, take a deep breath and notice what you are thinking and feeling.

3. Decide if that answer is a hot response (i.e., does it stir up an unpleasant memory, cause a strong feeling, or cause you to start an argument within yourself?).

4. At the end of each answer is the question, "Is this a hot response?" followed by a place to answer "yes" or "no." Check "yes" if the statement is a hot response. Check "no" if the statement is not a hot response.

Writing the Second New Sentence Stem

Select one hot response from the sentences you just completed and write a new sentence stem using that response. Refer to the instructions for writing the first sentence stem if you need to.

1. The hot response I want to work with is...

_____

_____

2. The new sentence stem is ...

_____

_____

Sentence Completion #3

Instructions: Write your new sentence stem in the space below:

_____

Complete that sentence stem with a different answer at least ten times. Ignore the yes or no answers at the end of each line. You will complete those answers in the next part of the exercise.

Is this a
hot response?

1. _____ ☐ Yes ☐ No

_____

2. _____ ☐ Yes ☐ No

_____

3. _____ ☐ Yes ☐ No

_____

4. _____ ☐ Yes ☐ No

_____

5. _____ ☐ Yes ☐ No

_____

6. _____ ☐ Yes ☐ No

_____

7. _____ ☐ Yes ☐ No

_____

8. _____ ☐ Yes ☐ No

_____

9. _____ ☐ Yes ☐ No

_____

10. _____ ☐ Yes ☐ No

Hot Responses

Instructions:

1. Read the list of answers that you have just written.

2. As you read each answer, take a deep breath and notice what you are thinking and feeling.

3. Decide if that answer is a hot response (i.e., does it stir up an unpleasant memory, cause a strong feeling, or cause you to start an argument within yourself?).

4. At the end of each answer is the question, "Is this a hot response?" followed by a place to answer "yes" or "no." Check "yes" if the statement is a hot response. Check "no" if the statement is not a hot response.

Final Sentence Completion

Instructions: Complete the following sentence stem with a different answer at least ten times. There are no right or wrong answers and it is okay to write things that are unusual, silly, or don't make sense. Relax and let yourself write whatever pops into your mind. Ignore the yes or no answers at the end of each line. You will complete those answers in the next part of the exercise.

"I am now becoming aware that..."

Is this a hot response?

1. _____ ☐ Yes ☐ No

_____

2. _____ ☐ Yes ☐ No

_____

3. _____ ☐ Yes ☐ No

_____

4. _____ ☐ Yes ☐ No

_____

5. _____ ☐ Yes ☐ No

_____

6. _____ ☐ Yes ☐ No

_____

7. _____ ☐ Yes ☐ No

_____

8. _____ ☐ Yes ☐ No

_____

9. _____ ☐ Yes ☐ No

_____

10. _____ ☐ Yes ☐ No

_____

Hot Responses

Instructions:

1. Read the list of answers that you have just written.

2. As you read each answer, take a deep breath and notice what you are thinking and feeling.

3. Decide if that answer is a hot response (i.e., does it stir up an unpleasant memory, cause a strong feeling, or cause you to start an argument within yourself?).

4. At the end of each answer is the question, "Is this a hot response?" followed by a place to answer "yes" or "no." Check "yes" if the statement is a hot response. Check "no" if the statement is not a hot response.

Finding Hidden Warning Signs

Select one hot response from the sentences you just completed and write a new sentence stem using that response. Refer to the instructions for writing the first sentence stem if you need to.

1. Review all four sentence completion exercises.

2. Read each answer that you marked as a hot response.

3. Read through your warning sign cards and see if there is a warning sign that describes that hot response.

    A. If there is, go on to the next hot response.

    B. If there is no warning sign card describing that hot response, write a new warning sign card, place it in the appropriate sequence with the other warning sign cards, and then go on to the next hot response.

E X E R C I S E
16
The Final Warning Sign List

1. **Arrange the Cards in Order:** Using the summary titles, arrange your packet of Warning Sign Identification Cards in the order that you believe they typically occur.

2. **Eliminate Duplication:** Eliminate duplication of warning signs by removing cards that have the same or similar titles. (At this point, you may have 30 or more cards with summary titles.)

3. **Back Track to Early Warning Signs:** Look at the first warning sign on the list and ask if there are any warning signs that occurred before this. If there are new warning signs, fill out a new warning sign card for each one.

4. **Identifying Relapse Justifications:** Look at the last card and ask yourself if there are any warning signs that occur between the last warning sign listed and the time you start to use addictively. If there are new warning signs, fill out a new warning sign card for each one. Be sure to identify the specific thoughts you use to convince yourself that it is okay to return to addictive use.

5. **Telling Your Relapse Story:** Tell the story of your relapse progression by sorting through the cards in order and describe each warning sign. If new memories or thoughts come to mind, talk about them.

6. **Getting Feedback about Hidden Warning Signs:** Ask those listening to help you identify any gaps in the action that may contain hidden warning signs. If new warning signs are discovered, fill out new cards and place them in the appropriate place in the sequence.

7. **Numbering the Cards:** Number the cards in the correct sequence by placing a number in the upper right-hand corner of each card. This will allow you to reconstruct the sequence easily after you sort the cards as required in the next steps.

8. **Checking for Completeness:**

    A. **Gaps in the Action:** Assure that there are no gaps in the action. A gap in the action is any missing step in a sequence of events. To identify a gap in the action read each warning sign and imagine yourself doing the sequence of activities. If you get to the point where you can't see in your own mind exactly how you got from one step to the next, a gap in the action exists. If there are gaps in the action, new warning sign cards need to be developed to fill in the gap.

    B. **Backtracking:** Assure that warning signs have been backtracked to the earliest warning sign that you are able to identify. To backtrack the first warning sign, ask yourself the question, "What happened that caused this warning sign to occur?" Write a new warning sign card and then ask yourself, "What happened that caused this warning sign to occur?" Keep going until you can't think of any new warning signs.

    C. **Relapse Justifications:** Be sure the last several warning signs identify how you justify, in your own mind, going back to alcohol or drug use.

9. **The Final Warning Sign List:** Copy the summary titles and descriptions from the relapse prevention cards to the Final Warning Sign List. (Do not fill out the section after each warning sign title that says "Critical: [] Yes [] No." You will receive instructions on how to complete those questions in the next section.)

The Final Warning Sign List

Warning Sign #1: _____ Critical? ☐ Yes ☐ No

Description: I know I am in trouble with my recovery when...

_____

_____

_____

_____

Warning Sign #2: _____ Critical? ☐ Yes ☐ No

Description: I know I am in trouble with my recovery when...

_____

_____

_____

_____

Warning Sign #3: _____ Critical? ☐ Yes ☐ No

Description: I know I am in trouble with my recovery when...

_____

_____

_____

_____

Warning Sign #4: _____ Critical? ☐ Yes ☐ No

Description: I know I am in trouble with my recovery when...

_____

_____

_____

_____

Warning Sign #5: _____ Critical? ☐ Yes ☐ No

Description: I know I am in trouble with my recovery when...

_____

_____

_____

_____

Warning Sign #6: _____ Critical? ☐ Yes ☐ No

Description: I know I am in trouble with my recovery when...

_____

_____

_____

_____

Warning Sign #7: _____ Critical? ☐ Yes ☐ No

Description: I know I am in trouble with my recovery when...

_____

_____

_____

_____

Warning Sign #8: _____ Critical? ☐ Yes ☐ No

Description: I know I am in trouble with my recovery when...

_____

_____

_____

_____

Warning Sign #9: _____ Critical? ☐ Yes ☐ No

Description: I know I am in trouble with my recovery when...

_____

_____

_____

_____

Warning Sign #10: _____ Critical? ☐ Yes ☐ No

Description: I know I am in trouble with my recovery when...

_____

_____

_____

_____

Warning Sign #11: _____ Critical? ☐ Yes ☐ No

Description: I know I am in trouble with my recovery when...

_____

_____

_____

_____

Warning Sign #12: _____ Critical? ☐ Yes ☐ No

Description: I know I am in trouble with my recovery when...

_____

_____

_____

_____

Warning Sign #13: _____ Critical? ☐ Yes ☐ No

Description: I know I am in trouble with my recovery when...

_____

_____

_____

_____

Warning Sign #14: _____ Critical? ☐ Yes ☐ No

Description: I know I am in trouble with my recovery when...

_____

_____

_____

_____

Warning Sign #15: _____ Critical? ☐ Yes ☐ No

Description: I know I am in trouble with my recovery when...

_____

_____

_____

_____

Warning Sign #16: _____ Critical? ☐ Yes ☐ No

Description: I know I am in trouble with my recovery when...

_____

_____

_____

_____

Warning Sign #17: _____ Critical? ☐ Yes ☐ No
Description: I know I am in trouble with my recovery when...

_____

_____

_____

_____

Warning Sign #18: _____ Critical? ☐ Yes ☐ No
Description: I know I am in trouble with my recovery when...

_____

_____

_____

_____

Warning Sign #19: _____ Critical? ☐ Yes ☐ No
Description: I know I am in trouble with my recovery when...

_____

_____

_____

_____

Warning Sign #20: _____ Critical? ☐ Yes ☐ No
Description: I know I am in trouble with my recovery when...

_____

_____

_____

_____

E X E R C I S E
17-A
Identifying Critical Warning Signs

Developed by Terence T. Gorski

Instructions: Critical warning signs are those that you can identify early and manage differently in order to avoid relapse. To identify your critical warning signs:

1. Review your final warning sign list and identify a warning sign which begins early in the relapse process that you will be able to easily recognize and intervene upon.

2. If you believe that a warning sign is a critical warning sign, check "Yes" after the word "Critical," which follows the warning sign title.

3. If you don't believe it is a critical warning, check "No."

4. Your goal is to identify at least three critical warning signs and list them below.

Critical Warning Sign #1: _____

Why I selected it: _____

_____

_____

Critical Warning Sign #2: _____

Why I selected it: _____

_____

_____

Critical Warning Sign #3: _____

Why I selected it: _____

_____

_____

17-B
Managing Critical Warning Sign #1

Developed by Terence T. Gorski

1. **Critical Warning Sign #1:** What is the first critical warning sign that you selected?

   _____

2. **High-Risk Situations (HRS):** Describe a situation that has activated this critical warning sign in the past.

   _____

   _____

   _____

   _____

   _____

   _____

   _____

   _____

3. **Thoughts:** What did you think after the warning sign was activated?

   _____

   _____

   _____

   _____

   _____

   _____

4. **Feelings:** What did you feel after the warning sign was activated?

_____

_____

_____

5. **Action Urges:** What did you have an urge to do after the warning sign was activated?

_____

_____

_____

6. **Coping Behavior:** What did you actually do to manage the warning sign?

_____

_____

_____

7. **Anticipated Outcome:** What did you want the coping behavior to accomplish?

_____

_____

_____

8. **Actual Outcome:** What actually happened when you used the coping behavior?

_____

_____

_____

9. **Intervention Points:** Where could you have used different thoughts, feelings, and actions to produce a better outcome?

    Intervention Point #1: The point where I could have done something different near the beginning of the experience is...

    _____

    _____

    _____

    Intervention Point #2: The point where I could have done something different in the middle of the experience is ...

    _____

    _____

    _____

    Intervention Point #3: The point where I could have done something different near the end of the experience is ...

    _____

    _____

    _____

10. **First Reconstruction:**

    A. What could I have done differently at the third intervention point?

    _____

    _____

    _____

    B. How would this have changed the outcome?

    _____

    _____

    _____

11. **Second Reconstruction:**

A. What could I have done differently at the second intervention point?

_____

_____

_____

B. How would this have changed the outcome?

_____

_____

_____

12. **Third Reconstruction:**

A. What could I have done differently at the first intervention point?

_____

_____

_____

B. How would this have changed the outcome?

_____

_____

_____

17-C
Managing Critical Warning Sign #2

Developed by Terence T. Gorski

1. **Critical Warning Sign #2:** What is the second critical warning sign that you selected?

    _____

2. **High-Risk Situations (HRS):** Describe a situation that has activated this critical warning sign in the past.

    _____

    _____

    _____

    _____

    _____

    _____

    _____

3. **Thoughts:** What did you think after the warning sign was activated?

    _____

    _____

    _____

    _____

    _____

    _____

4.   **Feelings:** What did you feel after the warning sign was activated?

_____

_____

_____

5.   **Action Urges:** What did you have an urge to do after the warning sign was activated?

_____

_____

_____

6.   **Coping Behavior:** What did you actually do to manage the warning sign?

_____

_____

_____

7.   **Anticipated Outcome:** What did you want the coping behavior to accomplish?

_____

_____

_____

8.   **Actual Outcome:** What actually happened when you used the coping behavior?

_____

_____

_____

9. **Intervention Points:** Where could you have used different thoughts, feelings, and actions to produce a better outcome?

Intervention Point #1: The point where I could have done something different near the beginning of the experience is...

_____

_____

_____

Intervention Point #2: The point where I could have done something different in the middle of the experience is ...

_____

_____

_____

Intervention Point #3: The point where I could have done something different near the end of the experience is ...

_____

_____

_____

10. **First Reconstruction:**

A. What could I have done differently at the third intervention point?

_____

_____

_____

B. How would this have changed the outcome?

_____

_____

_____

11. **Second Reconstruction:**

A. What could I have done differently at the second intervention point?

_____

_____

_____

B. How would this have changed the outcome?

_____

_____

_____

12. **Third Reconstruction:**

A. What could I have done differently at the first intervention point?

_____

_____

_____

B. How would this have changed the outcome?

_____

_____

_____

17-D
Managing Critical Warning Sign #3

Developed by Terence T. Gorski

1. **Critical Warning Sign #3:** What is the third critical warning sign that you selected?

    _____

2. **High-Risk Situations (HRS):** Describe a situation that has activated this critical warning sign in the past.

    _____

    _____

    _____

    _____

    _____

    _____

    _____

3. **Thoughts:** What did you think after the warning sign was activated?

    _____

    _____

    _____

    _____

    _____

    _____

4. **Feelings:** What did you feel after the warning sign was activated?

_____

_____

_____

5. **Action Urges:** What did you have an urge to do after the warning sign was activated?

_____

_____

_____

6. **Coping Behavior:** What did you actually do to manage the warning sign?

_____

_____

_____

7. **Anticipated Outcome:** What did you want the coping behavior to accomplish?

_____

_____

_____

8. **Actual Outcome:** What actually happened when you used the coping behavior?

_____

_____

_____

9. **Intervention Points:** Where could you have used different thoughts, feelings, and actions to produce a better outcome?

Intervention Point #1: The point where I could have done something different near the beginning of the experience is...

_____

_____

_____

Intervention Point #2: The point where I could have done something different in the middle of the experience is ...

_____

_____

_____

Intervention Point #3: The point where I could have done something different near the end of the experience is ...

_____

_____

_____

10. **First Reconstruction:**

A. What could I have done differently at the third intervention point?

_____

_____

_____

B. How would this have changed the outcome?

_____

_____

_____

166

11. **Second Reconstruction:**

   A. What could I have done differently at the second intervention point?

   _____

   _____

   _____

   B. How would this have changed the outcome?

   _____

   _____

   _____

12. **Third Reconstruction:**

   A. What could I have done differently at the first intervention point?

   _____

   _____

   _____

   B. How would this have changed the outcome?

   _____

   _____

   _____

PART 3

Managing
Warning Signs

18
Filling Out the Back of
the Warning Sign
Identification Cards

Instructions: Now it is time to take your stack of Warning Sign Identification Cards and complete the following steps:

1. **Number the cards:** The cards are now arranged in the order in which your warning signs tend to occur. In a moment you will sort them in a different order. By numbering the cards in the upper right-hand corner, you will be able to put them back in the correct sequence quickly. Take a moment to number the cards now.

2. **Look at the back of a card**: You will notice that it starts with the phrase, "When this warning sign occurs, I tend to ...", followed by a space to identify what you tend to think, feel, and have an urge to do when you experience the warning sign.

3. **Fill out the back of all the cards**: Take a few moments to fill out the back of all the cards. Be sure that each blank space is filled by a short word or phrase that is concise and complete. For example:

   When I experience this warning sign, I tend to ...

   Think: I am no good.

   Feel: Ashamed and angry at myself.

   Have an urge to: Be by myself.

Note: Be sure to fill out the back of each card completely. You will need to use the completed cards in the next sequence of exercises.

E X E R C I S E
19
High-Risk Thought List

Developed by Terence T. Gorski

Instructions:

1. **Review high-risk thoughts:** Review the thought section of your relapse warning sign cards to be sure there is a thought statement written on the back of each card.

2. **Sort cards on thoughts**: Sort the cards in a way that eliminates duplication by putting the cards together that have the same or similar thoughts. You may, for example, have these three thoughts: "I am no good!"; "I am not worth anything!"; and "I am a horrible person!" These three thoughts are essentially the same. They all deal with telling yourself that you are no good. Because of this, these cards should be stacked on the same pile.

3. **Find three primary high-risk thoughts**: Select the three primary thoughts that drive the relapse warning signs. These usually represent the three biggest piles of cards.

4. **Write your high-risk thought list:** In the space provided on the high-risk thought list, write your three major high-risk thoughts that you identified by sorting your warning sign identification cards by thoughts.

5. **Rational alternatives**: Write another way that you could start to think that would support your sobriety and lower your risk of relapse. Write that new way of thinking in the second column of the high-risk thought list.

6. **Example**: The following is an example of how to complete the high-risk thought list:

Primary Irrational Thoughts that Lead to Relapse	Rational Alternative Thoughts (New Ways of Thinking to Prevent Relapse)
1. I have to work hard and accomplish more than I am required to.	1. I don't have to work hard all the time. I can set reasonable work goals.

Primary Irrational Thoughts that Lead to Relapse	Rational Alternative Thoughts (New Ways of Thinking to Prevent Relapse)
1. _____ _____ _____ _____ _____	1. _____ _____ _____ _____ _____
2. _____ _____ _____ _____ _____	2. _____ _____ _____ _____ _____
3. _____ _____ _____ _____	3. _____ _____ _____ _____

E X E R C I S E
20-A
High-Risk Feeling List

Developed by Terence T. Gorski

Instructions:

1. **Review unmanageable feelings:** Review the feeling section of your relapse warning sign cards to be sure there is a feeling statement written on the back of each card.

2. **Sort cards on feelings:** Sort the cards in a way that eliminates duplication by putting the cards together that have the same or similar feelings. For example, cards that say you are angry, mad, and hostile are all essentially the same and should be placed in a single pile to eliminate duplications.

3. **Write your initial feeling list:** In the space provided below write the three major feelings that you identified by sorting your warning sign identification cards by feelings.

High-Risk Feeling #1: _____

High-Risk Feeling #2: _____

High-Risk Feeling #3: _____

20-B
The Feeling List
Worksheet

4. **Review the following list of feelings:** Check any feelings that have either activated relapse warning signs or caused you to feel an urge to start using addictively.

☐ **Strength:** I feel strong. I am experiencing high energy, power, and potency.

☐ **Weakness:** I feel weak. I am experiencing low energy, frailty, and impotence.

☐ **Anger:** I feel angry. I am experiencing agitation, displeasure, and hostility.

☐ **Caring:** I feel caring. I am experiencing emotional warmth that makes me want to protect, nurture, or care for someone or something.

☐ **Joy:** I feel joyful. I am experiencing excitement because I know that I have something of value or anticipate receiving something of value.

☐ **Sorrow:** I feel sad. I am experiencing anguish, grief, and regret.

☐ **Security:** I feel secure. I am experiencing a sense of stability, peace of mind, and assurance caused by the conviction that I am safe and in no danger.

☐ **Fear:** I feel scared. I am experiencing a sense of uneasiness and agitation caused by the conviction that I am in danger or at risk.

☐ **Frustration:** I feel frustrated. I am experiencing a sense of agitation caused by the inability to achieve a desired goal.

☐ **Fulfillment:** I feel fulfilled. I am experiencing an inner sense of satisfaction caused by the achieving or believing that I will achieve a desired goal.

Exaggerated and Distorted Feelings: The following feelings are exaggerations or distortions of the ten primary healthy feelings listed above. These feelings are created by a primary feeling plus an irrational thought that either exaggerates, minimizes, or distorts the primary feeling.

☐ **Grandiosity:** I feel grandiose. I am experiencing an inner sense of extreme strength and power caused by the conviction that it is impossible for anyone or anything to defeat me. (Grandiosity is an exaggeration of strength.)

☐ **Helplessness:** I feel helpless. I am experiencing an extreme sense of weakness caused by the conviction that I am so powerless that I am unable to defend or take care of myself. (Helplessness is an exaggeration of weakness.)

☐ **Resentment:** I feel resentful. I am experiencing a sense of intense anger and hostility that will not go away or diminish. (Resentment is an exaggeration of anger.)

☐ **Obligation:** I feel obligated. I have such a strong sense of caring that I believe I must neglect or sacrifice myself in order to demonstrate that I care. (Obligation is an exaggeration of caring.)

☐ **Mania:** I feel manic. I am so overjoyed that I am experiencing a sense of intoxication and agitated delight. (Mania is an exaggeration of joy.)

☐ **Depression:** I feel depressed. I am so sorrowful, anguished, and grief stricken that I am having difficulty functioning normally. (Depression is an exaggeration of sadness.)

☐ **Complacency:** I feel complacent. I feel so secure and satisfied that I have lost my sense of motivation. (Complacency is an exaggeration of security.)

☐ **Panic:** I feel panic. I am so afraid that something terrible will happen that I have difficulty functioning well. (Panic is an exaggeration of fear.)

☐ **Hopeless:** I feel hopeless. I am experiencing severe frustration caused by the conviction that I will never be able to get what I want or need. (Hopelessness is an exaggeration of frustration.)

☐ **Bored:** I feel boredom. I am feeling such a strong sense of inner contentment that I have difficulty in motivating myself to do things that I need to do. (Boredom is an exaggeration of fulfillment.)

☐ **Guilt:** I feel guilty. I have a deep-seated sense of remorse because I know I have done something wrong. (Guilt can be a healthy response to violating a personal value, an exaggeration of sadness, or the result of an irrational judgment that I have done something wrong.)

☐ **Shame:** I feel a sense of shame because I am convinced that "I am defective as a person!" (Shame is an exaggeration of guilt caused by the belief that I am defective as a person and incapable of improving.)

5. Compare with warning sign identification cards: Compare this list to the three primary high-risk feelings that surfaced from sorting your cards. If there are other high-risk feelings that you became aware of enter them below.

High-Risk Feeling #4: _____

High-Risk Feeling #5: _____

High-Risk Feeling #6: _____

6. **Find three primary high-risk feelings:** Select the three feelings that put you at highest risk of relapse from the six feelings you have previously identified.

1st Highest-Risk Feeling: _____

2nd Highest-Risk Feeling:_____

3rd Highest-Risk Feeling: _____

7. **Enter on the feeling management worksheet:** Enter these three feelings on the Feeling Management Worksheet in the first column.

8. Feeling mismanagement: Write a brief sentence for each describing how the feeling was mismanaged under the name of the feeling in column one of the Feeling Management Worksheet.

9. **Feeling management strategy:** In the second column of the Feeling Management Worksheet, write a better way of managing or resolving the feeling.

10. **Example:** The following is an example of how to complete the High-Risk Feeling List.

Primary Unmanageable Feeling and Ways of Mismanaging It that Lead to Relapse	New and More Effective Feeling Management Strategy to Prevent Relapse
1. Feeling: Anger	1. Notice when I am angry.
How I mismanage it....	Identify who or what I am angry at.
Pretend everything is okay and refuse to admit to myself or anyone else that I am angry.	Talk about my anger with a safe person.
	Talk about it with the person I am angry with.

20-C
Feeling Management
Worksheet

Developed by Terence T. Gorski

Primary Unmanageable Feelings and Ways of Mismanaging Them that Lead to Relapse	New and More Effective Feeling Management Strategy to Prevent Relapse
1. Feeling:	1.
How I mismanage it...	
2. Feeling:	2.
How I mismanage it...	
3. Feeling:	3.
How I mismanage it...	

E X E R C I S E
21
High-Risk Action List

Developed By Terence T. Gorski

1.   Review self-defeating actions: Review the action section of your relapse warning sign cards to be sure there is an action statement written on the back of each card.

2.   **Sort cards on actions:** Sort the cards in a way that eliminates duplication by putting the cards together that have the same or similar actions.

3.   **Find three primary self-defeating actions:** Select the three primary self-defeating actions that drive the relapse warning signs and write them in the appropriate place in column one of the High-Risk Action List. These usually represent the three biggest piles of cards.

   A.   **Action urges:** First write what you have an urge to do in the first column of the High-Risk Action Form where it says, "I have an urge to ...".

   B.   **Old coping behavior:** Under the action urge, write the old way in which you would have actually behaved where it says, "What I actually do is ...".

4.   **New and more effective actions:** In column two, write a new and more effective way of acting that can help you avoid relapse where it says, "What I can do instead ...".

5.   **Example:** The following is an example of how to complete the High-Risk Action List.

Primary Self-defeating Actions or Action Urges that Lead to Relapse	New and More Effective Actions (New Ways of Behaving) that Can Prevent Relapse
1. I have an urge to ... Yell, scream, and storm out of the room when I am angry. What I actually do is... Get quiet, become a nice guy, pretend everything is okay, isolate myself, and criticize myself for being a coward.	1. What I could do instead ... • Stop and notice my feelings. • Affirm it is okay to feel this way. • Decide if I want to deal with the issue or responsibly avoid it. • Decide if I want to deal with it now or later. • Discuss with safe person before putting into action.

High-Risk Action List

Developed by Terence T. Gorski

Primary Self-defeating Actions or Action Urges that Lead to Relapse	New and More Effective Actions (New Ways of Behaving) that Can Prevent Relapse
1. I have an urge to...	1. What I could do instead...
What I actually do is...	
2. I have an urge to...	2. What I could do instead...
What I actually do is...	
3. I have an urge to...	3. What I could do instead...
What I actually do is...	

E X E R C I S E
22
Identifying High-Risk Situations

Developed By Terence T. Gorski

A high-risk situation is any situation that is likely to activate a relapse warning sign or create an urge to start addictive use. There are many possible high-risk situations such as being around people who are using alcohol or drugs, getting fired or laid off, getting a divorce, having a serious accident, and so forth.

It is important to know what situations are likely to activate the urge to return to addictive use so you can create a plan for what you can do instead.

There are three ways to identify high-risk situations:

- Identify past situations that activated relapse warning signs or addictive use.

- Identify future situations that may activate relapse warning signs or addictive use.

- Identify situations that you are currently involved in that activate relapse warning signs or the desire to start addictive use.

Let's take a few moments to do all three.

22-A
Past High-Risk Situations

Instructions: Think of three past situations that activated relapse warning signs or caused you to return to addictive use. Briefly describe them below.

1. Past Situation #1:_____

_____

What are the chances that you will experience a situation like this within the next two to six weeks?

☐ Almost certain   ☐ High   ☐ Low   ☐ Very low

If you do experience a situation like this, what are the chances that you will start addictive use?

☐ Almost certain   ☐ High   ☐ Low   ☐ Very low

2. Past Situation #2:_____

_____

What are the chances that you will experience a situation like this within the next two to six weeks?

☐ Almost certain   ☐ High   ☐ Low   ☐ Very low

If you do experience a situation like this, what are the chances that you will start addictive use?

☐ Almost certain   ☐ High   ☐ Low   ☐ Very low

3. Past Situation #3:_____

_____

What are the chances that you will experience a situation like this within the next two to six weeks?

☐ Almost certain   ☐ High   ☐ Low   ☐ Very low

If you do experience a situation like this, what are the chances that you will start addictive use?

☐ Almost certain   ☐ High   ☐ Low   ☐ Very low

22-B
Future High-Risk Situations

Instructions: Think of three future situations that could activate relapse warning signs or cause you to return to addictive use. Briefly describe them below.

1. Future Situation #1: _____

_____

What are the chances that you will experience a situation like this within the next two to six weeks?

☐ Almost certain   ☐ High   ☐ Low   ☐ Very low

If you do experience a situation like this, what are the chances that you will start addictive use?

☐ Almost certain   ☐ High   ☐ Low   ☐ Very low

2. Future Situation #2: _____

_____

What are the chances that you will experience a situation like this within the next two to six weeks?

☐ Almost certain   ☐ High   ☐ Low   ☐ Very low

If you do experience a situation like this, what are the chances that you will start addictive use?

☐ Almost certain   ☐ High   ☐ Low   ☐ Very low

3. Future Situation #3: _____

_____

What are the chances that you will experience a situation like this within the next two to six weeks?

☐ Almost certain   ☐ High   ☐ Low   ☐ Very low

If you do experience a situation like this, what are the chances that you will start addictive use?

☐ Almost certain   ☐ High   ☐ Low   ☐ Very low

22-C
Current High-Risk Situations

Instructions: Think of three current situations that are activating your relapse warning signs or causing you to want to start addictive use. Briefly describe them below.

1. Current Situation #1: _____

_____

What are the chances that you will experience a situation like this within the next two to six weeks?

☐ Almost certain ☐ High ☐ Low ☐ Very low

If you do experience a situation like this, what are the chances that you will start addictive use?

☐ Almost certain ☐ High ☐ Low ☐ Very low

2. Current Situation #2: _____

_____

What are the chances that you will experience a situation like this within the next two to six weeks?

☐ Almost certain ☐ High ☐ Low ☐ Very low

If you do experience a situation like this, what are the chances that you will start addictive use?

☐ Almost certain ☐ High ☐ Low ☐ Very low

3. Current Situation #3: _____

_____

What are the chances that you will experience a situation like this within the next two to six weeks?

☐ Almost certain ☐ High ☐ Low ☐ Very low

If you do experience a situation like this, what are the chances that you will start addictive use?

☐ Almost certain ☐ High ☐ Low ☐ Very low

23
Managing High-Risk Situations

Developed by Terence T. Gorski

1. **Find three primary high-risk situations:** Select the three primary high-risk situations from the high-risk situation lists (past, future, and current) that you have developed in the previous exercise and write them in the appropriate place in column one of the High-Risk Action List.

2. **New low-risk situations:** In column two, write new low-risk situations that you can get involved in to avoid activating your warning signs or the thoughts, feelings, or actions (TFAs) that drive them.

3. **Example:** The following is an example of how to complete the High-Risk Situation List.

High-Risk Situation that Will Activate My Warning Signs or the Thoughts, Feelings, and Actions that Drive Them.	Other Situations I Can Get Involved in to Avoid Activating My Warning Signs or the Thoughts, Feelings, and Actions that Drive Them.
1. Socializing with people who are using alcohol or drugs regularly and heavily.	1. Going to AA meetings and socializing with sober people.

High-Risk Situations that Will Activate My Warning Signs or the Thoughts, Feelings, and Actions that Drive Them.

1. _____

_____

_____

_____

_____

2. _____

_____

_____

_____

_____

3. _____

_____

_____

_____

_____

Other Situations I Can Get Involved in to Avoid Activating My Warning Signs or the Thoughts, Feelings, and Actions that Drive Them.

1. _____

_____

_____

_____

_____

2. _____

_____

_____

_____

_____

3. _____

_____

_____

_____

_____

24-A
Identifying Mandate and Injunction #1
Developed by Terence T. Gorski

1. Copy the first primary irrational thought that drives your relapse warning signs from your High-Risk Thought List (Exercise 19).

    _____

    _____

    _____

2. Think about this irrational thought and ask yourself what this thought tells you that you must, ought to, or should think about, feel, or do. Write that statement below.

    I must ... _____

    _____

    _____

3. Think about what consequences you believe will happen if you don't do what this thought tells you that you must, ought to, or should do. Write those consequences below.

    Or else ... _____

    _____

    _____

4. Think about the first primary irrational thought again and ask yourself what that thought tells you that you cannot, must not, or should not do. Write this statement below.

    I must not ... _____

    _____

    _____

5. Think about what consequences you believe will happen if you do what this thought tells you that you must not, should not, or cannot do. Write those consequences below.

Or else ... _____

_____

_____

6. Mandate #1: Write the statements from questions 2 and 3 above in the correct places below.

I must ... _____

_____

_____

Or else ... _____

_____

_____

7. Injunction #1: Write the statements from questions 4 and 5 in the correct places below.

I cannot ... _____

_____

_____

Or else ... _____

_____

_____

24-B
Identifying Mandate and
Injunction #2
Developed by Terence T. Gorski

1. Copy the second primary irrational thought that drives your relapse warning signs from your High-Risk Thought List (Exercise 19).

    _____

    _____

    _____

2. Think about this irrational thought and ask yourself what this thought tells you that you must, ought to, or should think about, feel, or do. Write that statement below.

    I must ... _____

    _____

    _____

3. Think about what consequences you believe will happen if you don't do what this thought tells you that you must, ought to, or should do. Write those consequences below.

    Or else ... _____

    _____

    _____

4. Think about the second primary irrational thought again and ask yourself what that thought tells you that you cannot, must not, or should not do. Write this statement below.

    I must not ... _____

    _____

    _____

5. Think about what consequences you believe will happen if you do what this thought tells you that you must not, should not, or cannot do. Write those consequences below.

Or else ... _____

_____

_____

6. Mandate #2: Write the statements from questions 2 and 3 above in the correct places below.

I must ... _____

_____

_____

Or else ... _____

_____

_____

7. Injunction #2: Write the statements from questions 4 and 5 in the correct places below.

I cannot ... _____

_____

_____

Or else... _____

_____

_____

24-C
Identifying Mandate and Injunction #3
Developed by Terence T. Gorski

1. Copy the third primary irrational thought that drives your relapse warning signs from your High-Risk Thought List (Exercise 19).

    _____

    _____

    _____

2. Think about this irrational thought and ask yourself what this thought tells you that you must, ought to, or should think about, feel, or do. Write that statement below.

    I must ... _____

    _____

    _____

3. Think about what consequences you believe will happen if you don't do what this thought tells you that you must, ought to, or should do. Write those consequences below.

    Or else ... _____

    _____

    _____

4. Think about the third primary irrational thought again and ask yourself what that thought tells you that you cannot, must not, or should not do. Write this statement below.

    I must not ... _____

    _____

    _____

5. Think about what consequences you believe will happen if you do what this thought tells you that you must not, should not, or cannot do. Write those consequences below.

Or else ... _____

_____

_____

6. Mandate #3: Write the statements from questions 2 and 3 above in the correct places below.

I must ... _____

_____

_____

Or else ... _____

_____

_____

7. Injunction #3: Write the statements from questions 4 and 5 in the correct places below.

I cannot ... _____

_____

_____

Or else... _____

_____

_____

E X E R C I S E
24-D
Challenging Mandate and Injunction #1
Developed by Terence T. Gorski

1. **Mandate #1:** Write the first mandate that drives your relapse warning signs. (Select this mandate from Exercise 24-A, #6).

   I must_____

   _____

   _____

   Or else _____

   _____

   _____

2. **Challenging the mandate:**

   Who taught you that you must do this? _____

   _____

   Is it possible you were taught wrong?　☐ Yes　　☐ No

   Please explain: _____

   _____

   _____

   What are the benefits of continuing to act out this mandate?

   _____

   _____

   _____

What are the disadvantages of continuing to act out this mandate?

_____

_____

_____

If you continue to act out this mandate, what is the ...

*Best possible outcome?*_____

_____

Worst possible outcome? _____

_____

Most likely outcome? _____

_____

If you challenge this mandate and act differently, what is the ...

*Best possible outcome?*_____

_____

Worst possible outcome? _____

_____

Most likely outcome? _____

_____

3.   **Counteracting choice statement for the mandate:** What is another way of thinking about the mandate that will allow a choice between a sober response and an addictive response?

_____

_____

_____

4. **Primary injunction:** What is a primary injunction that drives your relapse warning signs? (Select this injunction from Exercise 24-A, #7).

I cannot _____

_____

Or else _____

5. **Challenging the injunction:**

Who taught you that you cannot do this? _____

_____

Is it possible you were taught wrong?　☐ Yes　　☐ No

Please explain: _____

_____

_____

_____

What are the benefits of continuing to act out this injunction?

_____

_____

_____

What are the disadvantages of continuing to act out this injunction?

_____

_____

_____

_____

If you continue to act in accordance with this injunction, what is the ...

*Best possible outcome?*_____

_____

Worst possible outcome? _____

_____

Most likely outcome? _____

_____

If you challenge this injunction and act differently, what is the ...

*Best possible outcome?*_____

_____

Worst possible outcome? _____

_____

Most likely outcome? _____

_____

6. **Counteracting choice statement for the injunction:** What is another way of thinking about the injunction that will allow a choice between a sober response and an addictive response?

_____

_____

_____

_____

24-E
Challenging Mandate
and Injunction #2
Developed by Terence T. Gorski

1. **Mandate #2:** Write the second mandate that drives your relapse warning signs. (Select this mandate from Exercise 24-B, #6.)

    I must_____

    _____

    _____

    Or else _____

    _____

    _____

2. **Challenging the mandate:**

    Who taught you that you must do this? _____

    _____

    Is it possible you were taught wrong?   ☐ Yes   ☐ No

    Please explain: _____

    _____

    _____

    What are the benefits of continuing to act out this mandate?

    _____

    _____

    _____

What are the disadvantages of continuing to act out this mandate?

_____

_____

_____

If you continue to act out this mandate, what is the ...

*Best possible outcome?*_____

_____

Worst possible outcome? _____

_____

Most likely outcome? _____

_____

If you challenge this mandate and act differently, what is the ...

*Best possible outcome?*_____

_____

Worst possible outcome? _____

_____

Most likely outcome? _____

_____

3. **Counteracting choice statement for the mandate:** What is another way of thinking about the mandate that will allow a choice between a sober response and an addictive response?

_____

_____

_____

4. **Primary injunction:** What is a primary injunction that drives your relapse warning signs? (Select this injunction from Exercise 24-B, #7.)

I cannot _____

_____

Or else _____

5. **Challenging the injunction:**

Who taught you that you cannot do this? _____

_____

Is it possible you were taught wrong? ☐ Yes ☐ No

Please explain: _____

_____

_____

_____

What are the benefits of continuing to act out this injunction?

_____

_____

_____

What are the disadvantages of continuing to act out this injunction?

_____

_____

_____

_____

If you continue to act in accordance with this injunction, what is the ...

*Best possible outcome?*_____

_____

Worst possible outcome? _____

_____

Most likely outcome? _____

_____

If you challenge this injunction and act differently, what is the ...

*Best possible outcome?*_____

_____

Worst possible outcome? _____

_____

Most likely outcome? _____

_____

6. **Counteracting choice statement for the injunction:** What is another way of thinking about the injunction that will allow a choice between a sober response and an addictive response?

_____

_____

_____

_____

_____

24-F
Challenging Mandate
and Injunction #3
Developed by Terence T. Gorski

1. **Mandate #3:** Write the third mandate that drives your relapse warning signs. (Select this mandate from Exercise 24-C, #6.)

    I must_____

    _____

    _____

    Or else _____

    _____

    _____

2. **Challenging the mandate:**

    Who taught you that you must do this? _____

    _____

    Is it possible you were taught wrong? ☐ Yes ☐ No

    Please explain: _____

    _____

    _____

    What are the benefits of continuing to act out this mandate?

    _____

    _____

    _____

What are the disadvantages of continuing to act out this mandate?

_____

_____

_____

If you continue to act out this mandate, what is the ...

*Best possible outcome?*_____

_____

Worst possible outcome? _____

_____

Most likely outcome? _____

_____

If you challenge this mandate and act differently, what is the ...

*Best possible outcome?*_____

_____

Worst possible outcome? _____

_____

*Most likely outcome?*_____

_____

3. **Counteracting choice statement for the mandate:** What is another way of thinking about the mandate that will allow a choice between a sober response and an addictive response?

_____

_____

_____

4. **Primary injunction:** What is a primary injunction that drives your relapse warning signs? (Select this injunction from Exercise 24-C, #7.)

I cannot _____

_____

Or else _____

5. **Challenging the injunction:**

Who taught you that you cannot do this? _____

_____

Is it possible you were taught wrong? ☐ Yes ☐ No

Please explain: _____

_____

_____

What are the benefits of continuing to act out this injunction?

_____

_____

_____

What are the disadvantages of continuing to act out this injunction?

_____

_____

_____

If you continue to act in accordance with this injunction, what is the ...

*Best possible outcome?*_____

_____

Worst possible outcome? _____

_____

Most likely outcome? _____

_____

If you challenge this injunction and act differently, what is the ...

*Best possible outcome?*_____

_____

Worst possible outcome? _____

_____

Most likely outcome? _____

_____

6. **Counteracting choice statement for the injunction:** What is another way of thinking about the injunction that will allow a choice between a sober response and an addictive response?

_____

_____

_____

_____

_____

P A R T 4

Recovery Planning

25
Initial Recovery Plan

Now that you have identified your critical warning signs and developed management strategies, it is time to develop a schedule of recovery activities that can assist you in identifying and managing the critical warning signs.

Recovery is like walking up a down escalator. There is no such thing as standing still. You will need to work every day at identifying your relapse warning signs and the thoughts, feelings, and actions that drive them. You must consciously use new ways of thinking, feeling, and acting.

This will be difficult because your addictive habits have been deeply ingrained into your personality. Without a daily schedule of recovery activities, you will relapse into old ways of thinking, managing your feelings, and acting. This will lead to getting involved in addiction-centered situations and a return to addictive use.

The following procedure will help you to develop an initial recovery plan, test it to be sure it deals with your critical warning signs, and revise and strengthen it so it can be effective in preventing relapse.

Initial Recovery Plan

Instructions: Think of a typical week and complete your recovery plan below by: (1) entering the day and time of scheduled recovery activities; (2) describing the recovery activity in the second column: and (3) describing the primary goal of that activity in preventing relapse.

Day	Recovery Activity	Relapse Prevention Goal
M		
T		
W		
T		
F		
S		
S		

E X E R C I S E
26
Testing the Recovery Plan

Instructions: In the first column below, list the titles of your relapse warning signs by copying them in the correct order from your Final Warning Sign List. Below each title indicate if this is a critical warning sign by checking "yes" or "no." In the second column, list all recovery activities from your recovery plan that have the primary focus of helping you to identify and manage that warning sign. Be sure to list only recovery activities that directly relate to the identification and management of the warning sign (i.e., AA attendance does not address the identification or management of a warning sign entitled "Arguments With Wife"!).

Relapse Warning Signs:
(Copy titles from cards)

Recovery Activity:
(Copy recovery activities
from the recovery plan that
specifically addresses
each warning sign)

1. _____

    Critical warning sign?

    ☐ Yes   ☐ No

2. _____

    Critical warning sign?

    ☐ Yes   ☐ No

3. _____

    Critical warning sign?

    ☐ Yes   ☐ No

4. _____

    Critical warning sign?

    ☐ Yes   ☐ No

5. _____   _____

   Critical warning sign?   _____

   ☐ Yes   ☐ No   _____

                                       _____

6. _____   _____

   Critical warning sign?   _____

   ☐ Yes   ☐ No   _____

                                       _____

7. _____   _____

   Critical warning sign?   _____

   ☐ Yes   ☐ No   _____

                                       _____

8. _____   _____

   Critical warning sign?   _____

   ☐ Yes   ☐ No   _____

                                       _____

9. _____   _____

   Critical warning sign?   _____

   ☐ Yes   ☐ No   _____

                                       _____

10. _____   _____

    Critical warning sign?   _____

    ☐ Yes   ☐ No   _____

                                       _____

11. _____

   Critical warning sign?

   ☐ Yes   ☐ No

_____
_____
_____
_____

12. _____

   Critical warning sign?

   ☐ Yes   ☐ No

_____
_____
_____
_____

13. _____

   Critical warning sign?

   ☐ Yes   ☐ No

_____
_____
_____
_____

14. _____

   Critical warning sign?

   ☐ Yes   ☐ No

_____
_____
_____
_____

15. _____

   Critical warning sign?

   ☐ Yes   ☐ No

_____
_____
_____
_____

16. _____

   Critical warning sign?

   ☐ Yes   ☐ No

_____
_____
_____
_____

27
Identifying Weaknesses in the Recovery Plan

Instructions:

1. Review Exercise 26, "Testing the Recovery Plan."

2. Identify warning signs that do not have a specific recovery activity associated with them.

   A. Identify critical warning signs with no management strategies first.

   B. Identify other warning signs with no management strategies.

3. List the title of these warning signs in order of importance in column one.

4. In column two, describe why you don't have a management strategy for each warning sign listed in column one.

5. Ask yourself if, after thinking about it, you have decided that you need to develop a recovery activity for each warning sign and check "Y" for yes or "N" for no after the question, "Recovery plan needed?"

Warning Signs without Recovery Activities
(Copy from Exercise 26,
"Testing the Recovery Plan")

Describe the Reasons Why There Are
No Recovery Activities for These
Warning Signs

1. _____   _____

   Critical warning sign?   _____

   ☐ Yes   ☐ No   _____

                                    Recovery plan needed?   ☐ Y   ☐ N

2. _____   _____

   Critical warning sign?   _____

   ☐ Yes   ☐ No   _____

                                    Recovery plan needed?   ☐ Y   ☐ N

3. _____   _____

   Critical warning sign?   _____

   ☐ Yes   ☐ No   _____

                                    Recovery plan needed?   ☐ Y   ☐ N

Warning Signs without Recovery Activities
(Copy from Exercise 26,
"Testing the Recovery Plan")

Describe the Reasons Why There Are
No Recovery Activities for These
Warning Signs

4. _____

   Critical warning sign?

   ☐ Yes   ☐ No

   _____
   _____
   _____

   Recovery plan needed?   ☐ Y   ☐ N

5. _____

   Critical warning sign?

   ☐ Yes   ☐ No

   _____
   _____
   _____

   Recovery plan needed?   ☐ Y   ☐ N

6. _____

   Critical warning sign?

   ☐ Yes   ☐ No

   _____
   _____
   _____

   Recovery plan needed?   ☐ Y   ☐ N

7. _____

   Critical warning sign?

   ☐ Yes   ☐ No

   _____
   _____
   _____

   Recovery plan needed?   ☐ Y   ☐ N

8. _____

   Critical warning sign?

   ☐ Yes   ☐ No

   _____
   _____
   _____

   Recovery plan needed?   ☐ Y   ☐ N

9. _____

   Critical warning sign?

   ☐ Yes   ☐ No

   _____
   _____
   _____

   Recovery plan needed?   ☐ Y   ☐ N

Warning Signs without Recovery Activities
(Copy from Exercise 26,
"Testing the Recovery Plan")

Describe the Reasons Why There Are
No Recovery Activities for These
Warning Signs

10. _____

    Critical warning sign?

    ☐ Yes   ☐ No

_____

_____

_____

Recovery plan needed?   ☐ Y   ☐ N

11. _____

    Critical warning sign?

    ☐ Yes   ☐ No

_____

_____

_____

Recovery plan needed?   ☐ Y   ☐ N

12. _____

    Critical warning sign?

    ☐ Yes   ☐ No

_____

_____

_____

Recovery plan needed?   ☐ Y   ☐ N

13. _____

    Critical warning sign?

    ☐ Yes   ☐ No

_____

_____

_____

Recovery plan needed?   ☐ Y   ☐ N

14. _____

    Critical warning sign?

    ☐ Yes   ☐ No

_____

_____

_____

Recovery plan needed?   ☐ Y   ☐ N

15. _____

    Critical warning sign?

    ☐ Yes   ☐ No

_____

_____

_____

Recovery plan needed?   ☐ Y   ☐ N

28
Final Recovery Plan Worksheet

Instructions: Construct a new final recovery plan by: (1) entering day and time of scheduled recovery activities for each day; (2) describing the recovery activity; and (3) describing the goal of that activity in preventing relapse.

Day	Recovery Activity	Relapse Prevention Goal
M		
T		
W		
T		
F		
S		
S		

29
Daily Inventories

Developed by Terence T. Gorski

Instructions: The first steps in learning to avoid relapse are identifying your relapse warning signs, developing management strategies, and developing a recovery program that will help you identify and manage them. Regular inventory work is a vital part of any relapse prevention program. Warning signs often develop unconsciously. In other words, we can experience warning signs and not be consciously aware of it. By using daily inventories, we can train ourselves to become aware of warning signs as they develop and make decisions to consciously use our warning sign management strategies.

The most effective inventory method is to conduct a planning inventory every morning and a review inventory every evening. The morning planning inventory helps you to plan your day to assure recovery activities are built in and that you approach the day alert for the presence of any relapse warning signs. The evening review inventory gives you the opportunity to review the activities of your day, evaluate if you stuck to your recovery program or if you experienced any warning signs, and gives you the opportunity to take positive action if it is necessary.

The following forms are recommended for use during your morning and evening inventory processes. It is recommended that you copy these forms and use them each day.

29-A
Daily Planning Guide

Day_____ Date_____ Time_____

Major Goals for Today:

☐ 1. _____

☐ 2. _____

☐ 3. _____

☐ 4. _____

☐ 5. _____

Recovery Tasks

☐ 1. _____

☐ 2. _____

☐ 3. _____

☐ 4. _____

☐ 5. _____

Daily Tasks

☐ 1. _____

☐ 2. _____

☐ 3. _____

☐ 4. _____

☐ 5. _____

☐ 6. _____

☐ 7. _____

☐ 8. _____

☐ 9. _____

☐ 10. _____

Daily Time Plan

A M

6:00 - 7:00 _____

7:00 - 8:00 _____

8:00 - 9:00 _____

9:00 - 10:00 _____

10:00 - 11:00 _____

11:00 - 12:00 _____

P M

12:00 - 1:00 _____

1:00 - 2:00 _____

2:00 - 3:00 _____

3:00 - 4:00 _____

4:00 - 5:00 _____

5:00 - 6:00 _____

E V E N I N G

_____

_____

_____

_____

_____

Notes: _____

EXERCISE
29-B
Evening Review Inventory

Day _____ Date _____ Time_____

1. **Personal and Professional Progress:**

   Did I make progress today toward the accomplishment of my personal and professional goals?

   ☐ Yes ☐ No ☐ Uncertain

   How do I feel about that progress? _____

   _____

2. **Personal and Professional Shortcomings:**

   Did I encounter problems today in making progress toward my personal and professional goals?

   ☐ Yes ☐ No ☐ Uncertain

   How do I feel about those problems? _____

   _____

3. **Active Warning Signs:**

   Did I experience warning signs of excessive stress or relapse?

   ☐ Yes ☐ No ☐ Uncertain

   What have I done to manage those warning signs?

   How do I feel about the presence of those warning signs? _____

   _____

4. **Decision about the Need for Outside Help:**

   Do I need to talk with someone about the events of the day?

   ☐ Yes ☐ No ☐ Uncertain

   Do I need outside help to deal with the problems or warning signs that I experienced today?

   ☐ Yes ☐ No ☐ Uncertain

   What feelings am I experiencing as I think about my need for outside help? _____

   _____

30
Recovery Program
Standard Recommendations

Instructions: The following questions are designed to help you plan your ongoing recovery. Eighteen key recovery recommendations are reviewed. Each standard recommendation is followed by three questions. Answer each question as honestly as you can.

1. **Professional Counseling:**

   A. **Belief in Need:** How strongly do you believe that you need to attend regular group and individual sessions in order to avoid relapse in the future?

   ☐ Very strongly   ☐ Not very strongly
   ☐ Strongly   ☐ Not at all strongly

   B. **Obstacles:** What obstacles are likely to prevent you from attending regular group and individual counseling sessions?

   _____

   _____

   C. **Likelihood:** How likely are you to attend regular group or individual counseling sessions in the future?

   ☐ Very likely   ☐ Not very likely
   ☐ Somewhat likely   ☐ Not at all likely

2. **Self-Help Groups:**

   A. **Belief in Need:** How strongly do you believe that you need to attend self-help groups in order to avoid relapse in the future?

   ☐ Very strongly   ☐ Not very strongly
   ☐ Strongly   ☐ Not at all strongly

   B. **Obstacles:** What obstacles are likely to prevent you from attending self-help groups?

   _____

   _____

   C. **Likelihood:** How likely are you to regularly attend self-help groups in the future?

   ☐ Very likely   ☐ Not very likely
   ☐ Somewhat likely   ☐ Not at all likely

3. **Sponsorship:**

A. **Belief in Need:** How strongly do you believe that you need sponsorship in order to avoid relapse in the future?

☐ Very strongly   ☐ Not very strongly
☐ Strongly   ☐ Not at all strongly

B. **Obstacles:** What obstacles are likely to prevent you from getting and using a sponsor?

_____

_____

C. **Likelihood:** How likely are you to have a sponsor with whom you talk on a regular basis in the future?

☐ Very likely   ☐ Not very likely
☐ Somewhat likely   ☐ Not at all likely

4. **Step Work:**

A. **Belief in Need:** How strongly do you believe that you need step work in order to avoid relapse in the future?

☐ Very strongly   ☐ Not very strongly
☐ Strongly   ☐ Not at all strongly

B. **Obstacles:** What obstacles are likely to prevent you from step work?

_____

_____

C. **Likelihood:** How likely are you to use step work in the future?

☐ Very likely   ☐ Not very likely
☐ Somewhat likely   ☐ Not at all likely

5. **Meal Plan:**

A. **Belief in Need:** How strongly do you believe that you need a meal plan in order to avoid relapse in the future?

☐ Very strongly   ☐ Not very strongly
☐ Strongly   ☐ Not at all strongly

B. **Obstacles:** What obstacles are likely to prevent you from a meal plan?

_____

_____

C. **Likelihood:** How likely are you to eat three well-balanced meals per day in the future?

☐ Very likely   ☐ Not very likely
☐ Somewhat likely   ☐ Not at all likely

6. **Avoiding Sugars:**

A. **Belief in Need:** How strongly do you believe that you need to avoid sugars in order to avoid relapse in the future?

☐ Very strongly   ☐ Not very strongly
☐ Strongly   ☐ Not at all strongly

B. **Obstacles:** What obstacles are likely to prevent you from avoiding sugars?

_____

_____

C. **Likelihood:** How likely are you to avoid foods high in sugars in the future?

☐ Very likely   ☐ Not very likely
☐ Somewhat likely   ☐ Not at all likely

7. **Avoiding Caffeine:**

A. **Belief in Need:** How strongly do you believe that you need to avoid caffeine in order to avoid relapse in the future?

☐ Very strongly   ☐ Not very strongly
☐ Strongly   ☐ Not at all strongly

B. **Obstacles:** What obstacles are likely to prevent you from avoiding beverages containing caffeine?

_____

_____

C. **Likelihood:** How likely are you to avoid beverages containing caffeine in the future?

☐ Very likely
☐ Somewhat likely

☐ Not very likely
☐ Not at all likely

8. **Avoiding Nicotine:**

A. **Belief in Need:** How strongly do you believe that you need to avoid nicotine in order to avoid relapse in the future?

☐ Very strongly
☐ Strongly

☐ Not very strongly
☐ Not at all strongly

B. **Obstacles:** What obstacles are likely to prevent you from avoiding nicotine?

_____

_____

C. **Likelihood:** How likely are you to avoid the use of nicotine (including cigarettes, cigars and smokeless tobacco) in the future?

☐ Very likely
☐ Somewhat likely

☐ Not very likely
☐ Not at all likely

9. **Regular Exercise:**

A. **Belief in Need:** How strongly do you believe that you need regular exercise in order to avoid relapse in   the future?

☐ Very strongly
☐ Strongly

☐ Not very strongly
☐ Not at all strongly

B. **Obstacles:** What obstacles are likely to prevent you from regular exercise?

_____

_____

C. **Likelihood:** How likely are you to exercise at least three times per week for a minimum period of 20 to 30 minutes (in a manner that is strenuous enough to make you breathe hard and begin to sweat) in the future?

☐ Very likely
☐ Somewhat likely

☐ Not very likely
☐ Not at all likely

10. **Relaxation Exercises:**

    A. **Belief in Need:** How strongly do you believe that you need relaxation exercises in order to avoid relapse in the future?

    ☐ Very strongly   ☐ Not very strongly
    ☐ Strongly   ☐ Not at all strongly

    B. **Obstacles:** What obstacles are likely to prevent you from relaxation exercises?

_____

_____

    C. **Likelihood:** How likely are you to use relaxation techniques to relax in the future?

    ☐ Very likely   ☐ Not very likely
    ☐ Somewhat likely   ☐ Not at all likely

11. **Prayer and Meditation:**

    A. **Belief in Need:** How strongly do you believe that you need prayer and meditation in order to avoid relapse in the future?

    ☐ Very strongly   ☐ Not very strongly
    ☐ Strongly   ☐ Not at all strongly

    B. **Obstacles:** What obstacles are likely to prevent you from prayer and meditation?

_____

_____

    C. **Likelihood:** How likely are you to use prayer and meditation to help you recover in the future?

    ☐ Very likely   ☐ Not very likely
    ☐ Somewhat likely   ☐ Not at all likely

12. **Talking with Others:**

    A. **Belief in Need:** How strongly do you believe that you need to talk with others in order to avoid relapse in the future?

    ☐ Very strongly   ☐ Not very strongly
    ☐ Strongly   ☐ Not at all strongly

B. **Obstacles:** What obstacles are likely to prevent you from talking with others?

_____

_____

C. **Likelihood:** How likely are you to talk to people about your life and ask for feedback in the future?

☐ Very likely
☐ Somewhat likely

☐ Not very likely
☐ Not at all likely

13. **Prompt Problem Solving:**

A. **Belief in Need:** How strongly do you believe that you need prompt problem solving in order to avoid relapse in the future?

☐ Very strongly
☐ Strongly

☐ Not very strongly
☐ Not at all strongly

B. **Obstacles:** What obstacles are likely to prevent you from prompt problem solving?

_____

_____

C. **Likelihood:** How likely are you to attempt to solve problems promptly as they come up in the future?

☐ Very likely
☐ Somewhat likely

☐ Not very likely
☐ Not at all likely

14. **Recreational Activities:**

A. **Belief in Need:** How strongly do you believe that you need recreational activities in order to avoid relapse in the future?

☐ Very strongly
☐ Strongly

☐ Not very strongly
☐ Not at all strongly

B. **Obstacles:** What obstacles are likely to prevent you from being involved in recreational activities?

_____

_____

C. **Likelihood:** How likely are you to schedule time for recreational activities in the future?

- ☐ Very likely
- ☐ Somewhat likely
- ☐ Not very likely
- ☐ Not at all likely

15. **Family Activities:**

A. **Belief in Need:** How strongly do you believe that you need family activities in order to avoid relapse in the future?

- ☐ Very strongly
- ☐ Strongly
- ☐ Not very strongly
- ☐ Not at all strongly

B. **Obstacles:** What obstacles are likely to prevent you from family activities?

_____

_____

C. **Likelihood:** How likely are you to schedule time for activities with your family in the future?

- ☐ Very likely
- ☐ Somewhat likely
- ☐ Not very likely
- ☐ Not at all likely

16. **Time with Friends:**

A. **Belief in Need:** How strongly do you believe that you need time with friends in order to avoid relapse in the future?

- ☐ Very strongly
- ☐ Strongly
- ☐ Not very strongly
- ☐ Not at all strongly

B. **Obstacles:** What obstacles are likely to prevent you from time with friends?

_____

_____

C. **Likelihood:** How likely are you to schedule time to spend with friends in the future?

- ☐ Very likely
- ☐ Somewhat likely
- ☐ Not very likely
- ☐ Not at all likely

17. **Reasonable Work Schedule:**

A. **Belief in Need:** How strongly do you believe that you need a reasonable work schedule in order to avoid relapse in the future?

☐ Very strongly   ☐ Not very strongly
☐ Strongly   ☐ Not at all strongly

B. **Obstacles:** What obstacles are likely to prevent you from a reasonable work schedule?

_____

_____

C. **Likelihood:** How likely are you to work on a regular schedule that doesn't interfere with recreational or recovery activities in the future?

☐ Very likely   ☐ Not very likely
☐ Somewhat likely   ☐ Not at all likely

18. **Quiet Time:**

A. **Belief in Need:** How strongly do you believe that you need quiet time in order to avoid relapse in the future?

☐ Very strongly   ☐ Not very strongly
☐ Strongly   ☐ Not at all strongly

B. **Obstacles:** What obstacles are likely to prevent you from quiet time?

C. **Likelihood:** How likely are you to schedule some quiet time to think and plan your recovery program in the future?

☐ Very likely   ☐ Not very likely
☐ Somewhat likely   ☐ Not at all likely

30-A
Recovery Goals Worksheet

1. **Personal Goals:** Please identify three personal characteristics that need to be changed if you are to avoid relapse.

(A) _____

_____

(B) _____

_____

(C) _____

_____

2. **Occupational Goals:** Please identify the three major work-related problems that need to be resolved if you are to avoid relapse.

(A) _____

_____

(B) _____

_____

(C) _____

_____

3. **Family Goals:** Please identify the three major family problems that need to be resolved if you are to avoid relapse.

(A) _____

_____

(B) _____

_____

(C) _____

_____

4. **Social Goals:** Please identify the three major social problems that need to be resolved if you are to avoid relapse.

(A) _____

_____

(B) _____

_____

(C) _____

_____

5. **Twelve Step Goals:** Please identify the three major problems you have had in working your Twelve Step program that will need to be resolved if you are to avoid relapse.

(A) _____

_____

(B) _____

_____

(C) _____

_____

31
Weekly Planning Guide

Instructions: A weekly planning guide is designed to help you plan your regular recovery program at least four weeks in advance. The following weekly planning guides will allow you to enter all of your recovery activities for each week to help you plan ahead.

Name _____

Week beginning: _____

WEEKLY PLANNING GUIDE

	Monday	Tuesday	Wednesday	Thursday	Friday	Saturday	Sunday
7-8 AM							
8-9 AM							
9-10 AM							
10-11 AM							
11-12 AM							
12-1 PM							
1-2 PM							
2-3 PM							
3-4 PM							
4-5 PM							
5-6 PM							
EVENING							

Name _____

Week beginning: _____

WEEKLY PLANNING GUIDE

	Monday	Tuesday	Wednesday	Thursday	Friday	Saturday	Sunday
7-8 AM							
8-9 AM							
9-10 AM							
10-11 AM							
11-12 AM							
12-1 PM							
1-2 PM							
2-3 PM							
3-4 PM							
4-5 PM							
5-6 PM							
EVENING							

Name _____

Week beginning: _____

WEEKLY PLANNING GUIDE

	Monday	Tuesday	Wednesday	Thursday	Friday	Saturday	Sunday
7-8 AM							
8-9 AM							
9-10 AM							
10-11 AM							
11-12 AM							
12-1 PM							
1-2 PM							
2-3 PM							
3-4 PM							
4-5 PM							
5-6 PM							
EVENING							

Name _____

Week beginning: _____

WEEKLY PLANNING GUIDE

	Monday	Tuesday	Wednesday	Thursday	Friday	Saturday	Sunday
7-8 AM							
8-9 AM							
9-10 AM							
10-11 AM							
11-12 AM							
12-1 PM							
1-2 PM							
2-3 PM							
3-4 PM							
4-5 PM							
5-6 PM							
EVENING							

Name _____

Week beginning: _____

WEEKLY PLANNING GUIDE

	Monday	Tuesday	Wednesday	Thursday	Friday	Saturday	Sunday
7-8 AM							
8-9 AM							
9-10 AM							
10-11 AM							
11-12 AM							
12-1 PM							
1-2 PM							
2-3 PM							
3-4 PM							
4-5 PM							
5-6 PM							
EVENING							

How to Build a
Relapse Prevention Network

By Terence T. Gorski

Relapse prevention planning is most effective when you develop a network of family members, friends, and fellow Twelve Step members who are willing to help you stay sober. These people make a commitment to learn about your recovery plans and relapse warning signs. They also agree to support your efforts at recovery while confronting any relapse into warning signs or addictive use.

It is important to choose the members of your relapse prevention network carefully. Not all people want to be involved and not everyone who wants involvement will be able to help you. You should involve people who are...

- Sober and have a solid recovery program or people who have never had a drinking or drug problem.

- Knowledgeable about chemical dependence as a disease or are willing to learn about the disease and recovery.

- Supportive of your need for abstinence.

- Supportive of relapse prevention planning as part of your recovery plan.

You **should not** involve people who are ...

- Chemically dependent and actively using alcohol or other drugs (this includes heavy drinkers or illegal drug users who deny they are addicted).

- Not informed about chemical dependency as a disease and are not willing to learn about it.

- Not supportive of your need for abstinence.

- Not supportive of relapse prevention planning as part of your recovery plan.

Members of your relapse prevention network must be willing to make commitments, not only to helping you recover but also to practicing a program of personal recovery. Remember, your addiction has affected everyone who has been involved with you. There are rarely exceptions. The family members, close personal friends, employers, even fellow associates in Alcoholics Anonymous have probably been damaged by your progressive relapse history. Their involvement in your relapse prevention network can help them recover from this damage if they are willing to work cooperatively with you to understand and overcome the obstacles that lead to relapse.

Participation in a relapse prevention network is demanding. Unless your friends and family members are involved in their own recovery program, it is not a good idea to ask them to become involved in your relapse prevention network. Until they can resolve their own problems with codependence, they will not be in a good position to help you. Trying to help you stay sober may cause their codependency to progress if they do not have a recovery program of their own. It is important to remember that codependents love to control chemically dependent people and "make them recover." These codependent attitudes are not helpful to interrupting the chronic relapse process.

Some members of Alanon become concerned when they are invited to be part of a relapse prevention network. They mistakenly feel that such involvement violates the Alanon program of recovery. This is not true. Detachment from the symptoms of addictive disease is a big part of Alanon, but detachment does not mean abandonment.

If you do relapse, your loved ones will have to cope with the situation. By working with you to plan a course of action, the Alanon members can detach with love while taking the necessary steps to protect themselves and others from the consequence of the relapse. They can also learn how to encourage you to seek treatment without trying to control or force you to do so. Codependents can learn to give honest and accurate feedback about relapse warning signs and can take prompt and effective action to encourage the chemically dependent person to seek treatment without violating their own Alanon recovery programs.

The basic goal of involving significant others in your relapse prevention plan is to identify and change the ineffective ways of communicating about your warning signs. What typically happens is that you experience a warning sign and start to act it out. The person you are with reacts to your warning signs in a way that triggers additional warning signs. As you act out the new warning signs, they continue to respond in a way that pushes you farther and farther toward relapse. In order to interrupt this process, you must take responsibility for changing the communication pattern by openly talking with others about effective ways to deal with you when you are acting out your warning signs.

There are six steps in building a relapse prevention network:

Step 1: Decide who you want to be involved and enter their names on the **Significant Other List**.

Step 2: Complete a **Significant Other Evaluation Form** for each person on that list and decide if this person is appropriate for involvement.

Step 3: Complete a **Significant Other Worksheet** for each person on the evaluation form.

Step 4: Meet with each person privately. Bring your **Final Warning Sign List** and the completed **Significant Other Worksheet** with you. Explain that you would like to discuss your problem of relapse with them and ask them to help you in the future.

Step 5: Review your **Final Warning Sign List** with the person and ask for feedback and reactions.

Step 6: Discuss your answers to each question on the **Significant Other Worksheet** with him or her.

Step 7: Schedule a series of meetings with all members of your relapse prevention network to discuss your progress and problems in recovery.

E X E R C I S E
32
The Significant Other List

Developed by Terence T. Gorski, 1985

Instructions: List the people you would like to get involved in your relapse prevention network, their relationship with you, and why you want them to be involved.

Person #1: _____ Relationship: _____

Why do you want him or her involved?

_____

_____

_____

_____

Person #2: _____ Relationship: _____

Why do you want him or her involved?

_____

_____

_____

_____

Person #3: _____ Relationship: _____

Why do you want him or her involved?

_____

_____

_____

_____

Person #4: _____ Relationship: _____

Why do you want him or her involved?

_____

_____

_____

_____

Person #5: _____ Relationship: _____

Why do you want him or her involved?

_____

_____

_____

_____

E X E R C I S E
33-A
Significant Other Evaluation Form #1

Developed by Terence T. Gorski, 1985

Instructions: Answer the following questions about each person on your **Significant Other List** to determine if they are appropriate members of your relapse prevention network.

==

Person #1: _____

Relationship: _____

Does he or she...

1.	Believe that chemical dependency is a disease?	☐ Yes	☐ No
2.	Support your efforts to abstain from alcohol and other mood-altering drugs?	☐ Yes	☐ No
3.	Support your use of relapse prevention planning as part of your recovery program?	☐ Yes	☐ No
4.	Use alcohol or other mood-altering drugs heavily or regularly?	☐ Yes	☐ No
5.	Practice a personal recovery program for chemical addiction?	☐ Yes	☐ No
6.	Practice a personal recovery program for codependency?	☐ Yes	☐ No
7.	Did you discuss the prospect of involving this person with your counselor or sponsor?	☐ Yes	☐ No

Please summarize his/her comments: _____

_____

_____

_____

8. Is he/she appropriate for involvement in my relapse
prevention network? .... ☐ Yes ☐ No

Why? _____

_____

_____

33-B
Significant Other Evaluation Form #2

Developed by Terence T. Gorski, 1985

Instructions: Answer the following questions about each person on your **Significant Other List** to deter-mine if they are appropriate members of your relapse prevention network.

==

Person #2: _____

Relationship: _____

Does he or she...

1.	Believe that chemical dependency is a disease?	☐ Yes	☐ No
2.	Support your efforts to abstain from alcohol and other mood-altering drugs?	☐ Yes	☐ No
3.	Support your use of relapse prevention planning as part of your recovery program?	☐ Yes	☐ No
4.	Use alcohol or other mood-altering drugs heavily or regularly?	☐ Yes	☐ No
5.	Practice a personal recovery program for chemical addiction?	☐ Yes	☐ No
6.	Practice a personal recovery program for codependency?	☐ Yes	☐ No
7.	Did you discuss the prospect of involving this person with your counselor or sponsor?	☐ Yes	☐ No

Please summarize his/her comments: _____

_____

_____

_____

8.	Is he/she appropriate for involvement in my relapse prevention network?	☐ Yes	☐ No

Why? _____

_____

_____

E X E R C I S E
33-C
Significant Other Evaluation Form #3

Developed by Terence T. Gorski, 1985

Instructions: Answer the following questions about each person on your **Significant Other List** to determine if they are appropriate members of your relapse prevention network.

===

Person #3: _____

Relationship: _____

Does he or she...

1. Believe that chemical dependency is a disease? .... ☐ Yes ☐ No
2. Support your efforts to abstain from alcohol and other mood-altering drugs? .... ☐ Yes ☐ No
3. Support your use of relapse prevention planning as part of your recovery program? .... ☐ Yes ☐ No
4. Use alcohol or other mood-altering drugs heavily or regularly? .... ☐ Yes ☐ No
5. Practice a personal recovery program for chemical addiction? .... ☐ Yes ☐ No
6. Practice a personal recovery program for codependency? .... ☐ Yes ☐ No
7. Did you discuss the prospect of involving this person with your counselor or sponsor? .... ☐ Yes ☐ No

Please summarize his/her comments: _____

_____

_____

_____

8. Is he/she appropriate for involvement in my relapse prevention network? .... ☐ Yes ☐ No

Why? _____

_____

_____

33-D
Significant Other Evaluation Form #4

Developed by Terence T. Gorski, 1985

Instructions: Answer the following questions about each person on your **Significant Other List** to determine if they are appropriate members of your relapse prevention network.

==

Person #4: _____

Relationship: _____

Does he or she...

1.	Believe that chemical dependency is a disease?	☐ Yes	☐ No
2.	Support your efforts to abstain from alcohol and other mood-altering drugs?	☐ Yes	☐ No
3.	Support your use of relapse prevention planning as part of your recovery program?	☐ Yes	☐ No
4.	Use alcohol or other mood-altering drugs heavily or regularly?	☐ Yes	☐ No
5.	Practice a personal recovery program for chemical addiction?	☐ Yes	☐ No
6.	Practice a personal recovery program for codependency?	☐ Yes	☐ No
7.	Did you discuss the prospect of involving this person with your counselor or sponsor?	☐ Yes	☐ No

Please summarize his/her comments: _____

_____

_____

_____

8.	Is he/she appropriate for involvement in my relapse prevention network?	☐ Yes	☐ No

Why? _____

_____

_____

==

E X E R C I S E
33-E
Significant Other Evaluation Form #5

Developed by Terence T. Gorski, 1985

Instructions: Answer the following questions about each person on your **Significant Other List** to determine if they are appropriate members of your relapse prevention network.

==

Person #5: _____

Relationship: _____

Does he or she...

1.	Believe that chemical dependency is a disease?	☐ Yes	☐ No
2.	Support your efforts to abstain from alcohol and other mood-altering drugs?	☐ Yes	☐ No
3.	Support your use of relapse prevention planning as part of your recovery program?	☐ Yes	☐ No
4.	Use alcohol or other mood-altering drugs heavily or regularly?	☐ Yes	☐ No
5.	Practice a personal recovery program for chemical addiction?	☐ Yes	☐ No
6.	Practice a personal recovery program for codependency?	☐ Yes	☐ No
7.	Did you discuss the prospect of involving this person with your counselor or sponsor?	☐ Yes	☐ No

Please summarize his/her comments: _____

_____

_____

_____

8.	Is he/she appropriate for involvement in my relapse prevention network?	☐ Yes	☐ No

Why? _____

_____

_____

34
Significant Other Worksheets

Instructions:

The following worksheets are designed to help you, the relapse-prone person, to evaluate the reactions that both you and each significant other have when you are experiencing relapse warning signs. The goal is to identify things that you and the other person do that make the warning signs worse. With this information, you can begin to develop new ways of talking about and reacting to the warning signs that will help prevent relapse.

Complete a worksheet for each significant other before you talk with him or her.

In the next section, you will find a series of similar worksheets that you will give to each significant other to help them do the same type of evaluation about your reactions.

By comparing your responses, you can begin to talk about important issues that can help you prevent relapse in the future.

E X E R C I S E
34-A
Significant Other Worksheet #1

Developed by Terence T. Gorski, 1985

1. **Name of Significant Other:** _____

    Relationship: _____

2. **Triggers for Warning Signs:** What does this person say or do that triggers or activates your relapse warning signs?

    _____

    _____

    _____

    _____

3. **Relapse Warning Signs:** What relapse warning signs do you experience most often when you are around this person? (Select from your Final Warning Sign List.)

    A. Warning Sign #__: _____

    B. Warning Sign #__: _____

    C. Warning Sign #__: _____

    D. Warning Sign #__: _____

    E. Warning Sign #__: _____

4. **Effect on Other Person:** When you are experiencing these warning signs, how does it usually affect this person?

    _____

    _____

    _____

    _____

    _____

5. **Reaction to You**: How does this person usually react to you when you are experiencing these warning signs?

_____

_____

_____

_____

6. **Effect on You**: How does this person's reaction to your warning signs affect you?

_____

_____

_____

_____

7. **Effect on Your Recovery**: How does this person's reaction usually affect your recovery?

☐ Helps my recovery   ☐ Hurts my recovery
☐ Does not help or hurt my recovery

Please explain your answer.

_____

_____

_____

_____

8. **Your Response**: How do you usually respond to this person's reaction to your warning signs?

_____

_____

_____

_____

_____

9. **Effect on Your Recovery**: How does your response usually affect your recovery?

☐ Helps my recovery   ☐ Hurts my recovery
☐ Does not help or hurt my recovery

Please explain your answer.

_____

_____

_____

_____

_____

10. **Preferred Reaction**: How could this person react to your warning signs in a more helpful way?

_____

_____

_____

_____

_____

11. **Denial Interruption Plan**: What do you want the other person to do if you continue to act out the warning signs after they react to you in your preferred way?

_____

_____

_____

_____

_____

12. **Reaction to Addictive Use**: How did this person react in the past when you returned to addictive use?

_____

_____

_____

_____

_____

13. **Relapse Intervention Plan**: What do you want this person to do if you return to addictive use in the future?

_____

_____

_____

_____

_____

E X E R C I S E
34-B
Significant Other Worksheet #2

Developed by Terence T. Gorski, 1985

1. **Name of Significant Other:** _____

    Relationship: _____

2. **Triggers for Warning Signs**: What does this person say or do that triggers or activates your relapse warning signs?

    _____

    _____

    _____

    _____

3. **Relapse Warning Signs**: What relapse warning signs do you experience most often when you are around this person? (Select from your Final Warning Sign List.)

    A. Warning Sign #__: _____

    B. Warning Sign #__: _____

    C. Warning Sign #__: _____

    D. Warning Sign #__: _____

    E. Warning Sign #__: _____

4. **Effect on Other Person**: When you are experiencing these warning signs, how does it usually affect this person?

    _____

    _____

    _____

    _____

    _____

5. **Reaction to You**: How does this person usually react to you when you are experiencing these warning signs?

_____

_____

_____

_____

_____

6. **Effect on You**: How does this person's reaction to your warning signs affect you?

_____

_____

_____

_____

_____

7. **Effect on Your Recovery**: How does this person's reaction usually affect your recovery?

☐ Helps my recovery   ☐ Hurts my recovery
☐ Does not help or hurt my recovery

Please explain your answer.

_____

_____

_____

_____

_____

8. **Your Response**: How do you usually respond to this person's reaction to your warning signs?

_____

_____

_____

_____

9. **Effect on Your Recovery**: How does your response usually affect your recovery?

☐ Helps my recovery   ☐ Hurts my recovery
☐ Does not help or hurt my recovery

Please explain your answer.

_____

_____

_____

_____

10. **Preferred Reaction**: How could this person react to your warning signs in a more helpful way?

_____

_____

_____

_____

11. **Denial Interruption Plan**: What do you want the other person to do if you continue to act out the warning signs after they react to you in your preferred way?

_____

_____

_____

_____

_____

_____

12. **Reaction to Addictive Use**: How did this person react in the past when you returned to addictive use?

_____

_____

_____

_____

_____

_____

13. **Relapse Intervention Plan**: What do you want this person to do if you return to addictive use in the future?

_____

_____

_____

_____

_____

_____

34-C
Significant Other Evaluation Worksheet #3

Developed by Terence T. Gorski, 1985

1. **Name of Significant Other:** _____

   Relationship: _____

2. **Triggers for Warning Signs**: What does this person say or do that triggers or activates your relapse warning signs?

   _____

   _____

   _____

3. **Relapse Warning Signs**: What relapse warning signs do you experience most often when you are around this person? (Select from your Final Warning Sign List.)

   A. Warning Sign #___: _____

   B. Warning Sign #___: _____

   C. Warning Sign #___: _____

   D. Warning Sign #___: _____

   E. Warning Sign #___: _____

4. **Effect on Other Person**: When you are experiencing these warning signs, how does it usually affect this person?

   _____

   _____

   _____

   _____

5. **Reaction to You**: How does this person usually react to you when you are experiencing these warning signs?

_____

_____

_____

_____

_____

6. **Effect on You**: How does this person's reaction to your warning signs affect you?

_____

_____

_____

_____

_____

7. **Effect on Your Recovery**: How does this person's reaction usually affect your recovery?

☐ Helps my recovery   ☐ Hurts my recovery
☐ Does not help or hurt my recovery

Please explain your answer.

_____

_____

_____

_____

_____

8. **Your Response**: How do you usually respond to this person's reaction to your warning signs?

_____

_____

_____

_____

9. **Effect on Your Recovery**: How does your response usually affect your recovery?

☐ Helps my recovery   ☐ Hurts my recovery
☐ Does not help or hurt my recovery

Please explain your answer.

_____

_____

_____

_____

_____

10. **Preferred Reaction**: How could this person react to your warning signs in a more helpful way?

_____

_____

_____

_____

_____

11. **Denial Interruption Plan**: What do you want the other person to do if you continue to act out the warning signs after they react to you in your preferred way?

_____

_____

_____

_____

_____

12. **Reaction to Addictive Use**: How did this person react in the past when you returned to addictive use?

_____

_____

_____

_____

_____

13. **Relapse Intervention Plan**: What do you want this person to do if you return to addictive use in the future?

_____

_____

_____

_____

_____

34-D
Significant Other Evaluation Worksheet #4

Developed by Terence T. Gorski, 1985

1. **Name of Significant Other:** _____

    Relationship: _____

2. **Triggers for Warning Signs**: What does this person say or do that triggers or activates your relapse warning signs?

    _____

    _____

    _____

3. **Relapse Warning Signs**: What relapse warning signs do you experience most often when you are around this person? (Select from your Final Warning Sign List.)

    A. Warning Sign #__: _____

    B. Warning Sign #__: _____

    C. Warning Sign #__: _____

    D. Warning Sign #__: _____

    E. Warning Sign #__: _____

4. **Effect on Other Person**: When you are experiencing these warning signs, how does it usually affect this person?

    _____

    _____

    _____

    _____

5. **Reaction to You**: How does this person usually react to you when you are experiencing these warning signs?

_____

_____

_____

_____

_____

6. **Effect on You**: How does this person's reaction to your warning signs affect you?

_____

_____

_____

_____

_____

7. **Effect on Your Recovery**: How does this person's reaction usually affect your recovery?

☐ Helps my recovery   ☐ Hurts my recovery
☐ Does not help or hurt my recovery

Please explain your answer.

_____

_____

_____

_____

_____

8. **Your Response**: How do you usually respond to this person's reaction to your warning signs?

_____

_____

_____

_____

9. **Effect on Your Recovery**: How does your response usually affect your recovery?

☐ Helps my recovery   ☐ Hurts my recovery
☐ Does not help or hurt my recovery

Please explain your answer.

_____

_____

_____

_____

10. **Preferred Reaction**: How could this person react to your warning signs in a more helpful way?

_____

_____

_____

_____

11. **Denial Interruption Plan**: What do you want the other person to do if you continue to act out the warning signs after they react to you in your preferred way?

_____

_____

_____

_____

_____

12. **Reaction to Addictive Use**: How did this person react in the past when you returned to addictive use?

_____

_____

_____

_____

_____

13. **Relapse Intervention Plan**: What do you want this person to do if you return to addictive use in the future?

_____

_____

_____

_____

_____

34-E
Significant Other Evaluation Worksheet #5

Developed by Terence T. Gorski, 1985

1. **Name of Significant Other:** _____

   Relationship: _____ _____

2. **Triggers for Warning Signs:** What does this person say or do that triggers or activates your relapse warning signs?

   _____

   _____

   _____

3. **Relapse Warning Signs:** What relapse warning signs do you experience most often when you are around this person? (Select from your Final Warning Sign List.)

   A. Warning Sign #__: _____

   B. Warning Sign #__: _____

   C. Warning Sign #__: _____

   D. Warning Sign #__: _____

   E. Warning Sign #__: _____

4. **Effect on Other Person:** When you are experiencing these warning signs, how does it usually affect this person?

   _____

   _____

   _____

   _____

5. **Reaction to You**: How does this person usually react to you when you are experiencing these warning signs?

_____

_____

_____

_____

_____

6. **Effect on You**: How does this person's reaction to your warning signs affect you?

_____

_____

_____

_____

_____

7. **Effect on Your Recovery**: How does this person's reaction usually affect your recovery?

☐ Helps my recovery   ☐ Hurts my recovery
☐ Does not help or hurt my recovery

Please explain your answer.

_____

_____

_____

_____

8. **Your Response**: How do you usually respond to this person's reaction to your warning signs?

_____

_____

_____

_____

9. **Effect on Your Recovery**: How does your response usually affect your recovery?

☐ Helps my recovery ☐ Hurts my recovery
☐ Does not help or hurt my recovery

Please explain your answer.

_____

_____

_____

_____

_____

10. **Preferred Reaction**: How could this person react to your warning signs in a more helpful way?

_____

_____

_____

_____

_____

11. **Denial Interruption Plan**: What do you want the other person to do if you continue to act out the warning signs after they react to you in your preferred way?

_____

_____

_____

_____

_____

_____

12. **Reaction to Addictive Use**: How did this person react in the past when you returned to addictive use?

_____

_____

_____

_____

_____

_____

13. **Relapse Intervention Plan**: What do you want this person to do if you return to addictive use in the future?

_____

_____

_____

_____

_____

_____

35
Evaluating Relapse-Prone Persons

Instructions:

The following worksheets are designed for the significant others of relapse-prone people. The purpose is to help them evaluate the reactions they have when the relapse-prone person is experiencing relapse warning signs. The goal is to identify things that the significant other and the relapse-prone person do that make the warning signs worse. With this information they can begin to develop new ways of talking about and reacting to the warning signs that will help prevent relapse.

Have each significant other complete a worksheet for the relapse-prone person. By comparing the responses of the relapse-prone person and the significant other, they can begin to talk about important issues that can help you prevent relapse in the future.

E X E R C I S E
35-A
Relapse-Prone Person Worksheet #1

Developed by Terence T. Gorski, 1985

1. **Name of Relapse-Prone Person:** _____

   Relationship: _____

2. **Triggers for Warning Signs**: What do you do that can trigger or activate relapse warning signs in this relapse-prone person?

   _____

   _____

   _____

3. **Relapse Warning Signs**: What relapse warning signs does the relapse-prone person experience most often when you are around him or her? (Select from your Final Warning Sign List.)

   A.   Warning Sign #__: _____

   B.   Warning Sign #__: _____

   C.   Warning Sign #__: _____

   D.   Warning Sign #__: _____

   E.   Warning Sign #__: _____

4. **Effect on You**: When the relapse-prone person is experiencing these warning signs, how does it usually affect you?

   _____

   _____

   _____

   _____

5.   **Your Reaction**: How do you usually react to this relapse-prone person when he or she is experiencing these warning signs?

_____

_____

_____

_____

_____

_____

6.   **Your Effect on Him or Her**: How do you think your reactions to this relapse-prone person's warning signs affect him or her?

_____

_____

_____

_____

_____

_____

7.   **Effect on Their Recovery**: How do you think your reaction usually affects this relapse-prone person's recovery?

☐ Helps his / her recovery   ☐ Hurts his / her recovery
☐ Does not help or hurt his / her recovery

Please explain your answer

_____

_____

_____

_____

_____

_____

8. **Relapse-Prone Person's Response**: How does the relapse-prone person usually respond to your reaction to his or her warning signs?

_____

_____

_____

_____

9. **Effect on Relapse-Prone Person's Recovery**: How do you think the reaction of the relapse-prone person affects his or her recovery?

☐ Helps his / her recovery   ☐ Hurts his / her recovery
☐ Does not help or hurt his / her recovery

Please explain your answer.

_____

_____

_____

_____

10. **Preferred Reaction**: How could you react to this person's warning signs in a more helpful way?

_____

_____

_____

_____

11. **Denial Interruption Plan**: What can you do if the relapse-prone person continues to act out the warning signs after you responded to him or her in the way they wanted you to?

_____

_____

_____

_____

_____

_____

12. **Reaction to Addictive Use**: How have you reacted in the past when the relapse-prone person returned to addictive use?

_____

_____

_____

_____

_____

_____

13. **Relapse Intervention Plan**: What can you do differently in the future if the relapse-prone person returns to addictive use?

_____

_____

_____

_____

_____

_____

35-B
Relapse-Prone Person Worksheet #2

Developed by Terence T. Gorski, 1985

1. **Name of Relapse-Prone Person:** _____

    Relationship: _____

2. **Triggers for Warning Signs**: What do you do that can trigger or activate relapse warning signs in this relapse-prone person?

    _____

    _____

    _____

3. **Relapse Warning Signs**: What relapse warning signs does the relapse-prone person experience most often when you are around him or her? (Select from your Final Warning Sign List.)

    A. Warning Sign #__: _____

    B. Warning Sign #__: _____

    C. Warning Sign #__: _____

    D. Warning Sign #__: _____

    E. Warning Sign #__: _____

4. **Effect on You**: When the relapse-prone person is experiencing these warning signs, how does it usually affect you?

    _____

    _____

    _____

    _____

5. **Your Reaction**: How do you usually react to this relapse-prone person when he or she is experiencing these warning signs?

_____

_____

_____

_____

_____

6. **Your Effect on Him or Her**: How do you think your reactions to this relapse-prone person's warning signs affect him or her?

_____

_____

_____

_____

_____

7. **Effect on Their Recovery**: How do you think your reaction usually affects this relapse-prone person's recovery?

☐ Helps his / her recovery   ☐ Hurts his / her recovery
☐ Does not help or hurt his / her recovery

Please explain your answer.

_____

_____

_____

_____

_____

8. **Relapse-Prone Person's Response**: How does the relapse-prone person usually respond to your reaction to his or her warning signs?

_____

_____

_____

_____

_____

9. **Effect on Relapse-Prone Person's Recovery**: How do you think the reaction of the relapse-prone person affects his or her recovery?

☐ Helps his / her recovery   ☐ Hurts his / her recovery
☐ Does not help or hurt his / her recovery

Please explain your answer.

_____

_____

_____

_____

_____

10. **Preferred Reaction**: How could you react to this person's warning signs in a more helpful way?

_____

_____

_____

_____

_____

11. **Denial Interruption Plan**: What can you do if the relapse-prone person continues to act out the warning signs after you responded to him or her in the way they wanted you to?

_____

_____

_____

_____

_____

12. **Reaction to Addictive Use**: How have you reacted in the past when the relapse-prone person returned to addictive use?

_____

_____

_____

_____

_____

13. **Relapse Intervention Plan**: What can you do differently in the future if the relapse-prone person returns to addictive use?

_____

_____

_____

_____

_____

35-C
Relapse-Prone Person Worksheet #3

Developed by Terence T. Gorski, 1985

1. **Name of Relapse-Prone Person:** _____

   Relationship: _____

2. **Triggers for Warning Signs**: What do you do that can trigger or activate relapse warning signs in this relapse-prone person?

   _____

   _____

   _____

3. **Relapse Warning Signs**: What relapse warning signs does the relapse-prone person experience most often when you are around him or her? (Select from your Final Warning Sign List.)

   A. Warning Sign #__: _____

   B. Warning Sign #__: _____

   C. Warning Sign #__: _____

   D. Warning Sign #__: _____

   E. Warning Sign #__: _____

4. **Effect on You**: When the relapse-prone person is experiencing these warning signs, how does it usually affect you?

   _____

   _____

   _____

   _____

5. **Your Reaction**: How do you usually react to this relapse-prone person when he or she is experiencing these warning signs?

_____

_____

_____

_____

_____

6. **Your Effect on Him or Her**: How do you think your reactions to this relapse-prone person's warning signs affect him or her?

_____

_____

_____

_____

_____

7. **Effect on Their Recovery**: How do you think your reaction usually affects this relapse-prone person's recovery?

☐ Helps his / her recovery   ☐ Hurts his / her recovery
☐ Does not help or hurt his / her recovery

Please explain your answer.

_____

_____

_____

_____

_____

8. **Relapse-Prone Person's Response**: How does the relapse-prone person usually respond to your reaction to his or her warning signs?

_____

_____

_____

_____

9. **Effect on Relapse-Prone Person's Recovery**: How do you think the reaction of the relapse-prone person affects his or her recovery?

☐ Helps his / her recovery   ☐ Hurts his / her recovery
☐ Does not help or hurt his / her recovery

Please explain your answer.

_____

_____

_____

_____

_____

10. **Preferred Reaction**: How could you react to this person's warning signs in a more helpful way?

_____

_____

_____

_____

_____

11. **Denial Interruption Plan**: What can you do if the relapse-prone person continues to act out the warning signs after you responded to him or her in the way they wanted you to?

_____

_____

_____

_____

_____

_____

12. **Reaction to Addictive Use**: How have you reacted in the past when the relapse-prone person returned to addictive use?

_____

_____

_____

_____

_____

_____

13. **Relapse Intervention Plan**: What can you do differently in the future if the relapse-prone person returns to addictive use?

_____

_____

_____

_____

_____

_____

E X E R C I S E
35-D
Relapse-Prone Person Worksheet #4

Developed by Terence T. Gorski, 1985

1.   **Name of Relapse-Prone Person:** _____

     Relationship: _____

2.   **Triggers for Warning Signs**: What do you do that can trigger or activate relapse warning signs in this relapse-prone person?

     _____

     _____

     _____

3.   **Relapse Warning Signs**: What relapse warning signs does the relapse-prone person experience most often when you are around him or her? (Select from your Final Warning Sign List.)

     A.   Warning Sign #__: _____

     B.   Warning Sign #__: _____

     C.   Warning Sign #__: _____

     D.   Warning Sign #__: _____

     E.   Warning Sign #__: _____

4.   **Effect on You**: When the relapse-prone person is experiencing these warning signs, how does it usually affect you?

     _____

     _____   _____

     _____

     _____

     _____

5. **Your Reaction**: How do you usually react to this relapse-prone person when he or she is experiencing these warning signs?

_____

_____

_____

_____

_____

6. **Your Effect on Him or Her**: How do you think your reactions to this relapse-prone person's warning signs affect him or her?

_____

_____

_____

_____

_____

7. **Effect on Their Recovery**: How do you think your reaction usually affects this relapse-prone person's recovery?

☐ Helps his / her recovery   ☐ Hurts his / her recovery
☐ Does not help or hurt his / her recovery

Please explain your answer.

_____

_____

_____

_____

_____

8. **Relapse-Prone Person's Response**: How does the relapse-prone person usually respond to your reaction to his or her warning signs?

_____

_____

_____

_____

_____

9. **Effect on Relapse-Prone Person's Recovery**: How do you think the reaction of the relapse-prone person affects his or her recovery?

☐ Helps his / her recovery   ☐ Hurts his / her recovery
☐ Does not help or hurt his / her recovery

Please explain your answer.

_____

_____

_____

_____

_____

10. **Preferred Reaction**: How could you react to this person's warning signs in a more helpful way?

_____

_____

_____

_____

_____

11. **Denial Interruption Plan**: What can you do if the relapse-prone person continues to act out the warning signs after you responded to him or her in the way they wanted you to?

_____

_____

_____

_____

_____

_____

12. **Reaction to Addictive Use**: How have you reacted in the past when the relapse-prone person returned to addictive use?

_____

_____

_____

_____

_____

_____

13. **Relapse Intervention Plan**: What can you do differently in the future if the relapse-prone person returns to addictive use?

_____

_____

_____

_____

_____

_____

E X E R C I S E
35-E
Relapse-Prone Person Worksheet #5

Developed by Terence T. Gorski, 1985

1.   **Name of Relapse-Prone Person:** _____

     Relationship: _____

2.   **Triggers for Warning Signs**: What do you do that can trigger or activate relapse warning signs in this relapse-prone person?

    _____

    _____

    _____

3.   **Relapse Warning Signs**: What relapse warning signs does the relapse-prone person experience most often when you are around him or her? (Select from your Final Warning Sign List.)

    A.   Warning Sign #__: _____

    B.   Warning Sign #__: _____

    C.   Warning Sign #__: _____

    D.   Warning Sign #__: _____

    E.   Warning Sign #__: _____

4.   **Effect on You**: When the relapse-prone person is experiencing these warning signs, how does it usually affect you?

    _____

    _____

    _____

    _____

5. **Your Reaction**: How do you usually react to this relapse-prone person when he or she is experiencing these warning signs?

_____

_____

_____

_____

_____

6. **Your Effect on Him or Her**: How do you think your reactions to this relapse-prone person's warning signs affect him or her?

_____

_____

_____

_____

_____

7. **Effect on Their Recovery**: How do you think your reaction usually affects this relapse-prone person's recovery?

☐ Helps his / her recovery   ☐ Hurts his / her recovery
☐ Does not help or hurt his / her recovery

Please explain your answer.

_____

_____

_____

_____

_____

8. **Relapse-Prone Person's Response**: How does the relapse-prone person usually respond to your reaction to his or her warning signs?

_____

_____

_____

_____

9. **Effect on Relapse-Prone Person's Recovery**: How do you think the reaction of the relapse-prone person affects his or her recovery?

☐ Helps his / her recovery   ☐ Hurts his / her recovery
☐ Does not help or hurt his / her recovery

Please explain your answer.

_____

_____

_____

_____

10. **Preferred Reaction**: How could you react to this person's warning signs in a more helpful way?

_____

_____

_____

_____

11. **Denial Interruption Plan:** What can you do if the relapse-prone person continues to act out the warning signs after you responded to him or her in the way they wanted you to?

_____

_____

_____

_____

_____

_____

12. **Reaction to Addictive Use:** How have you reacted in the past when the relapse-prone person returned to addictive use?

_____

_____

_____

_____

_____

_____

13. **Relapse Intervention Plan:** What can you do differently in the future if the relapse-prone person returns to addictive use?

_____

_____

_____

_____

_____

_____

36
Relapse Prevention Network Checklist

Developed by Terence T. Gorski, 1985

1. **Preparation**: Prepare by completing the following:

    ☐ **Select potential members**: Select the potential members for the relapse prevention network by entering their names and relationship to you on the Significant Other List.

    ☐ **Evaluate potential members**: Evaluate each potential member by completing a Significant Other Evaluation Form for each person you selected.

    ☐ **Discuss your evaluation**: Discuss these evaluations with your counselor or fellow AA members who are supportive of your developing a relapse prevention network with the goal of deciding who should be involved in the network.

    ☐ **Decide who to invite**: Decide who you will invite to join.

2. **First Private Conversation**: Talk with each potential member privately in order to invite them. Do the following in that first private conversation:

    ☐ Explain your need for their help in your recovery.

    ☐ Explain your recovery and relapse history.

    ☐ Make amends to the person for any harm your addiction or your relapse history may have caused.

    ☐ Explain that the relapse prevention group will meet three or four times for a period of one-and-a-half to two hours.

    ☐ Give the person a blank copy of the Significant Other Worksheet. Tell him or her that you will fill out this worksheet with your ideas and would like to discuss your answers with him or her in a second private conversation.

    ☐ Set the time and the date for the second private conversation.

3. **Complete Significant Other Worksheets**: Complete a Significant Other Worksheet for each person before your second private meeting. These worksheets ask you to identify the relapse warning signs you typically experience around that person, how he or she has reacted in the past, and how he or she can react in a more helpful way in the future.

4. **Second Private Conversation**: In the second private conversation, do the following:

    ☐ Ask the person if he or she had any reactions to your first conversation. Discuss how he or she thought and felt about your first meeting.

    ☐ Review the contents of the Significant Other Worksheet with the person.

☐ Ask if he or she agrees with your assessment.

☐ Discuss any disagreements and modify the answers on the form as necessary to assure you both understand and are in agreement with each other.

☐ Invite the person to meet with the other members of the network for a group meeting. Tell them the date, time, and location for the first group meeting.

☐ Tell them that the first meeting will be started by you asking everyone to introduce themselves and discuss why they agreed to be part of the network that's helping you prevent relapse.

☐ Get a firm commitment from them to attend the meeting.

5. **First Group Meeting**: Conduct the first group meeting using the following agenda:

☐ **Introductions**: Ask all members to introduce themselves and describe why they decided to become involved.

☐ **Briefly tell your story**: Briefly describe your recovery and relapse history. This should last no longer than ten minutes.

☐ **Explain each member's importance**: Describe why you selected each person and why each person is important to your recovery.

☐ **Briefly explain the recovery/relapse process**: Briefly explain the recovery and relapse process and the steps of relapse prevention planning. If necessary, lend them copies of the book, *Staying Sober: A Guide to Relapse Prevention*, to read.

☐ **Review your warning signs with the group**: Present your personal warning signs of relapse to the group one at a time. After presenting each warning sign, ask if anyone has questions, has anything to add, or has any problems with what they heard you say.

☐ **Get feedback from the members**: After all of the personal warning signs have been read, go around the circle and ask everyone to answer three questions:

    ☐ 1. Which warning signs do you believe I described correctly?

    ☐ 2. Which warning signs do you think I described inaccurately?

    ☐ 3. Can you think of any warning signs that should be added to the list?

☐ **Closure exercise**: Ask each member to share with the group his or her reaction to this session by describing what was learned and how he or she feels as a result of attending.

☐ **Refreshments**: Serve refreshments and socialize briefly.

☐ **Adjournment**: Set the time and place for the next meeting and adjourn.

6. **Review and Revise the Significant Other Worksheets**: Review and revise the significant other worksheets that you prepared earlier. There will probably be new information that came up in the first session that will change your previous responses.

7. **The Second Meeting:** Conduct the second meeting using the following agenda:

☐ **Reactions to last session**: Ask everyone to share their reactions to the last meeting. Go around the circle and ask everyone to comment. Be sure to ask people what they thought about the last meeting and how they felt about what happened.

☐ **Review of Significant Other Worksheets**: Review the questions on the Significant Other Worksheets one by one and discuss them in the group.

☐ **Keep notes:** Keep notes on what you learn from the comments and discussion.

☐ **Limit discussion time**: Limit the discussion to approximately 90 minutes. If necessary, schedule an extra meeting to review all worksheets.

☐ **Closure exercise**: Ask each member to share with the group his or her reaction to this session by describing what was learned and how he or she feels as a result of attending.

☐ **Refreshments**: Serve refreshments and socialize briefly.

☐ **Adjournment**: Set the time and place for the next meeting and adjourn.

8. **The Third Meeting**: Conduct the third meeting using the following agenda:

☐ **Reactions to last session**: Ask everyone to share their reactions to the last meeting. Go around the circle and ask everyone to comment. Be sure to ask people what they thought about the last meeting and how they felt about what happened.

☐ **Warning sign interruption plan**: Discuss what members are willing to do if you are showing relapse warning signs and refuse to listen to feedback or change your behavior.

☐ **Practice at warning sign interruption**: Have the group imagine that you have been showing a relapse warning sign for several weeks and have them pretend to confront you about what is happening. Discuss the strengths and weaknesses of the confrontation after the role-play is done. Remember, the goal is to be supportive yet directive. The love and caring must come through along with the rigorous honesty.

☐ **Relapse Early Intervention Plan**: Discuss what you want each member to do should you return to addictive use. Work together to design an early intervention plan which will put pressure on you to enter treatment should you return to addictive use.

☐ **Practice at relapse intervention**: Ask the group to imagine that you have returned to addictive use and they are meeting with you. Have them pretend to intervene upon you and see how well they handle it. Present some resistance or denial just to see how the group will handle this. Tell the group better ways that they can bypass your denial and pressure you to get into treatment.

☐ **Closure exercise**: Ask each member to share with the group his or her reaction to this session by describing what was learned and how he or she feels as a result of attending.

☐ **Refreshments**: Serve refreshments and socialize briefly.

☐ **Adjournment**: Set the time and place for the next meeting and adjourn.

9. **Follow-up Meeting:** Establish a follow-up meeting for one month later and a schedule to regularly talk with members at AA meetings, in personal visits, or over the telephone.

E X E R C I S E
37
Updating Your Relapse Prevention Planning

Developed by Terence T. Gorski

Instructions: As people progress in recovery, the warning signs that place them in risk of relapse change. Therefore, it is important for you to review and update your warning sign list and management strategies at regular intervals. We recommend a review every three months during the first year of sobriety, every six months for the second and third years of sobriety, and annually for the rest of your life. You can update your warning sign list by completing the following steps:

1. **Review your original personal warning sign list**: Read the personal warning sign list that you developed and place a check mark in front of the warning signs that still seem to fit your situation in recovery and an "X" in front of the warning signs that no longer seem to fit.

2. **Review your warning sign management strategies**: Review the warning sign management strategies that you developed. Include the management strategies for critical warning signs and high-risk thoughts, feelings, actions, and situations.

   A. Note the management strategies that you found helpful in dealing with your warning signs.

   B. Note the management strategies that you either never used or did not find helpful.

3. **Read the "Phases and Warning Signs of Relapse"**: Read the phases and warning signs of relapse again and see if any new warning signs stand out to you. If they do, go back to the initial warning sign list and the warning sign analysis procedures in the workbook and complete them for the new warning signs.

4. **Develop new management strategies**: Develop new management strategies for any new warning sign that you identified.

5. **Review your recovery program**: Review your recovery program and be sure there are recovery activities to support the identification and management of any new warning signs that you identified.

6. **Review your Relapse Early Intervention Plan**: Review your relapse early intervention plan to assure that the intervention strategies are still appropriate to your situation in life and your stage in recovery.

7. **Update members of your relapse prevention network**: Call the members of your relapse prevention network and tell them about the new warning signs, management strategies, and early intervention strategies you developed during the relapse prevention update session.

A Final Word

Congratulations!

If you have come this far, you have invested a great deal of time and energy into your relapse prevention plan. By this time, you should have learned new things about your own personal warning signs which have led you to past relapses. You also should have identified the weaknesses in your past recovery program that made you vulnerable for relapse. Finally, you should have developed new ways to identify and manage your relapse warning signs so that a return to addictive use becomes unnecessary.

It is important to remember that relapse prevention planning is never really over. A sponsor once told me to remember that this disease is called alcohol-*ism*, not alcohol-**wasm**. The disease doesn't go away. It lies dormant within us waiting to be awakened by some problem or stressor in our lives.

As we grow and develop in life and in our personal recovery, we will need to renew and update our relapse warning signs as well as our goals in recovery. There is a rule to recovery—we are either growing or we are dying. We are either recovering or setting ourselves up to relapse.

Relapse prevention therapy does not guarantee lifelong recovery, but it does increase your power of choice. Once you identify your early relapse warning signs, you can choose to take action to manage them before they grow into an uncontrollable nightmare that drives you back to addictive use.

Remember, you can recover if you use these methods on a daily basis in conjunction with ongoing involvement in other recovery programs. There is no such thing as a hopeless addict. There are only people who haven't learned about relapse prevention.

Good luck on your journey to sobriety!

Terence T. Gorski

Relapse Prevention Certification School

An Important Career Step in the Field of Chemical Dependency Counseling

The Relapse Prevention Certification School is the only training experience of its kind. Chemical Dependency professionals can gain an exclusive career advantage by becoming a Certified Relapse Prevention Specialist by participating in just six days of intensive training and demonstrating competency by completing a formal case study.

Two Classes Per Year in a Six-Day Format

Six-day training classes are held in both Spring and Fall in the Chicago area. Training focuses on professional and personal growth. Sessions consist of lectures and demonstrations of specific skills, role playing, and group exercises.

Program Goals

- Learn to assess, identify and manage relapse warning signs and plan a recovery program.
- Learn to apply proven new therapy techniques that will prevent relapse.

Who Should Attend

Professionals interested in developing expertise in Relapse Prevention Therapy.

- Program Managers
- CD Counselors
- Employee Assistance Counselors
- Private Practitioners
- Probation and Parole Counselors

Highly Trained Staff

Terence Gorski conducts the training with the assistance of twelve highly qualified instructors who work with groups no larger than eight.

A Specialized Skills Training Format

Training is presented in three one-hour segments which consist of a lecture and demonstration of a specific skill, a role play where participants experience both therapist and client roles, and a small group exercise to discuss progress and problems. Counseling and feedback are offered at the conclusion of each segment.

This unique format has been developed and field tested through consecutive classes since 1986. By focusing on professional and personal growth, our training prepares people for new opportunities in the field of relapse prevention therapy—as clinicians and program directors.

Clinical Director

Terence T. Gorski, MA, CAC, is president of The CENAPS Corporation, an organization which provides training, consultation, and research services for chemical dependency and behavioral health problems. He is Clinical Director of the Relapse Prevention Certification School.

A nationally and internationally recognized speaker, Terry Gorski has authored numerous books and articles on recovery and relapse prevention and has conducted training in the United States, Canada, and Europe. His practical approach is based on more than 30 years experience as a therapist, supervisor, program administrator and consultant.

For More Information and an Application for the Certification Program, Contact:
The CENAPS® Corporation
13194 Spring Hill Drive
Spring Hill, FL 34609
Phone: 352/596-8000 Fax: 352/596-8002

Warning Sign Identification Card—Side 1

Title: _____

Description: I know I'm in trouble with my recovery when I...

Thought: When I experience this warning sign I tend to think...

Feeling: When I experience this warning sign I tend to feel...

Urge: When I experience this warning sign I have an urge to...

Action: When I experience this warning sign what I actually do is...

Reaction: I tend to invite others to become part of my problem by...

For reorders call: Herald House/Independence Press at 1-800-767-8181 or (816) 521-3015

Warning Sign Identification Card—Side 1

Title: _____

Description: I know I'm in trouble with my recovery when I...

Thought: When I experience this warning sign I tend to think...

Feeling: When I experience this warning sign I tend to feel...

Urge: When I experience this warning sign I have an urge to...

Action: When I experience this warning sign what I actually do is...

Reaction: I tend to invite others to become part of my problem by...

For reorders call: Herald House/Independence Press at 1-800-767-8181 or (816) 521-3015

Warning Sign Identification Card—Side 1

Title: _____

Description: I know I'm in trouble with my recovery when I...

Thought: When I experience this warning sign I tend to think...

Feeling: When I experience this warning sign I tend to feel...

Urge: When I experience this warning sign I have an urge to...

Action: When I experience this warning sign what I actually do is...

Reaction: I tend to invite others to become part of my problem by...

For reorders call: Herald House/Independence Press at 1-800-767-8181 or (816) 521-3015

Warning Sign Identification Card—Side 1

Title: _____

Description: I know I'm in trouble with my recovery when I...

Thought: When I experience this warning sign I tend to think...

Feeling: When I experience this warning sign I tend to feel...

Urge: When I experience this warning sign I have an urge to...

Action: When I experience this warning sign what I actually do is...

Reaction: I tend to invite others to become part of my problem by...

For reorders call: Herald House/Independence Press at 1-800-767-8181 or (816) 521-3015

Warning Sign Identification Card—Side 2

Title:

Recovery Activities: The recovery activities I can use to manage this warning sign are…

Managing Thoughts: A new way of thinking that will help me manage this warning sign is…

Managing Feelings: A new way of managing my feelings is…

Managing Urges: A new way of managing my urges is…

Managing Actions: A new way of acting is…

Managing Reactions: A new way of inviting people to help me is…

Item #9780830913329

Warning Sign Identification Card—Side 2

Title:

Recovery Activities: The recovery activities I can use to manage this warning sign are…

Managing Thoughts: A new way of thinking that will help me manage this warning sign is…

Managing Feelings: A new way of managing my feelings is…

Managing Urges: A new way of managing my urges is…

Managing Actions: A new way of acting is…

Managing Reactions: A new way of inviting people to help me is…

© 1995 Terence T. Gorski CENAPS®

Item #9780830913329

Warning Sign Identification Card—Side 2

Title:

Recovery Activities: The recovery activities I can use to manage this warning sign are…

Managing Thoughts: A new way of thinking that will help me manage this warning sign is…

Managing Feelings: A new way of managing my feelings is…

Managing Urges: A new way of managing my urges is…

Managing Actions: A new way of acting is…

Managing Reactions: A new way of inviting people to help me is…

© 1995 Terence T. Gorski CENAPS®

Item #9780830913329

Warning Sign Identification Card—Side 2

Title:

Recovery Activities: The recovery activities I can use to manage this warning sign are…

Managing Thoughts: A new way of thinking that will help me manage this warning sign is…

Managing Feelings: A new way of managing my feelings is…

Managing Urges: A new way of managing my urges is…

Managing Actions: A new way of acting is…

Managing Reactions: A new way of inviting people to help me is…

© 1995 Terence T. Gorski CENAPS®

Item #9780830913329

Warning Sign Identification Card—Side 1

Title: _____

Description: I know I'm in trouble with my recovery when I...

Thought: When I experience this warning sign I tend to think...

Feeling: When I experience this warning sign I tend to feel...

Urge: When I experience this warning sign I have an urge to...

Action: When I experience this warning sign what I actually do is...

Reaction: I tend to invite others to become part of my problem by...

For reorders call: Herald House/Independence Press at 1-800-767-8181 or (816) 521-3015

Warning Sign Identification Card—Side 1

Title: _____

Description: I know I'm in trouble with my recovery when I...

Thought: When I experience this warning sign I tend to think...

Feeling: When I experience this warning sign I tend to feel...

Urge: When I experience this warning sign I have an urge to...

Action: When I experience this warning sign what I actually do is...

Reaction: I tend to invite others to become part of my problem by...

For reorders call: Herald House/Independence Press at 1-800-767-8181 or (816) 521-3015

Warning Sign Identification Card—Side 1

Title: _____

Description: I know I'm in trouble with my recovery when I...

Thought: When I experience this warning sign I tend to think...

Feeling: When I experience this warning sign I tend to feel...

Urge: When I experience this warning sign I have an urge to...

Action: When I experience this warning sign what I actually do is...

Reaction: I tend to invite others to become part of my problem by...

For reorders call: Herald House/Independence Press at 1-800-767-8181 or (816) 521-3015

Warning Sign Identification Card—Side 1

Title: _____

Description: I know I'm in trouble with my recovery when I...

Thought: When I experience this warning sign I tend to think...

Feeling: When I experience this warning sign I tend to feel...

Urge: When I experience this warning sign I have an urge to...

Action: When I experience this warning sign what I actually do is...

Reaction: I tend to invite others to become part of my problem by...

For reorders call: Herald House/Independence Press at 1-800-767-8181 or (816) 521-3015

Warning Sign Identification Card—Side 2

Title: _____

Recovery Activities: The recovery activities I can use to manage this warning sign are…

Managing Thoughts: A new way of thinking that will help me manage this warning sign is…

Managing Feelings: A new way of managing my feelings is…

Managing Urges: A new way of managing my urges is…

Managing Actions: A new way of acting is…

Managing Reactions: A new way of inviting people to help me is…

© 1995 Terence T. Gorski CENAPS®

Item #9780830913329

Warning Sign Identification Card—Side 2

Title: _____

Recovery Activities: The recovery activities I can use to manage this warning sign are…

Managing Thoughts: A new way of thinking that will help me manage this warning sign is…

Managing Feelings: A new way of managing my feelings is…

Managing Urges: A new way of managing my urges is…

Managing Actions: A new way of acting is…

Managing Reactions: A new way of inviting people to help me is…

© 1995 Terence T. Gorski CENAPS®

Item #9780830913329

Warning Sign Identification Card—Side 2

Title: _____

Recovery Activities: The recovery activities I can use to manage this warning sign are…

Managing Thoughts: A new way of thinking that will help me manage this warning sign is…

Managing Feelings: A new way of managing my feelings is…

Managing Urges: A new way of managing my urges is…

Managing Actions: A new way of acting is…

Managing Reactions: A new way of inviting people to help me is…

© 1995 Terence T. Gorski CENAPS®

Item #9780830913329

Warning Sign Identification Card—Side 2

Title: _____

Recovery Activities: The recovery activities I can use to manage this warning sign are…

Managing Thoughts: A new way of thinking that will help me manage this warning sign is…

Managing Feelings: A new way of managing my feelings is…

Managing Urges: A new way of managing my urges is…

Managing Actions: A new way of acting is…

Managing Reactions: A new way of inviting people to help me is…

© 1995 Terence T. Gorski CENAPS®

Item #9780830913329

Warning Sign Identification Card—Side 1

Title: _____

Description: I know I'm in trouble with my recovery when I...

Thought: When I experience this warning sign I tend to think...

Feeling: When I experience this warning sign I tend to feel...

Urge: When I experience this warning sign I have an urge to...

Action: When I experience this warning sign what I actually do is...

Reaction: I tend to invite others to become part of my problem by...

For reorders call: Herald House/Independence Press at 1-800-767-8181 or (816) 521-3015

Warning Sign Identification Card—Side 1

Title: _____

Description: I know I'm in trouble with my recovery when I...

Thought: When I experience this warning sign I tend to think...

Feeling: When I experience this warning sign I tend to feel...

Urge: When I experience this warning sign I have an urge to...

Action: When I experience this warning sign what I actually do is...

Reaction: I tend to invite others to become part of my problem by...

For reorders call: Herald House/Independence Press at 1-800-767-8181 or (816) 521-3015

Warning Sign Identification Card—Side 1

Title: _____

Description: I know I'm in trouble with my recovery when I...

Thought: When I experience this warning sign I tend to think...

Feeling: When I experience this warning sign I tend to feel...

Urge: When I experience this warning sign I have an urge to...

Action: When I experience this warning sign what I actually do is...

Reaction: I tend to invite others to become part of my problem by...

For reorders call: Herald House/Independence Press at 1-800-767-8181 or (816) 521-3015

Warning Sign Identification Card—Side 1

Title: _____

Description: I know I'm in trouble with my recovery when I...

Thought: When I experience this warning sign I tend to think...

Feeling: When I experience this warning sign I tend to feel...

Urge: When I experience this warning sign I have an urge to...

Action: When I experience this warning sign what I actually do is...

Reaction: I tend to invite others to become part of my problem by...

For reorders call: Herald House/Independence Press at 1-800-767-8181 or (816) 521-3015

Warning Sign Identification Card—Side 1

Title: _____

Description: I know I'm in trouble with my recovery when I...

Thought: When I experience this warning sign I tend to think...

Feeling: When I experience this warning sign I tend to feel...

Urge: When I experience this warning sign I have an urge to...

Action: When I experience this warning sign what I actually do is...

Reaction: I tend to invite others to become part of my problem by...

For reorders call: Herald House/Independence Press at 1-800-767-8181 or (816) 521-3015

Warning Sign Identification Card—Side 1

Title: _____

Description: I know I'm in trouble with my recovery when I...

Thought: When I experience this warning sign I tend to think...

Feeling: When I experience this warning sign I tend to feel...

Urge: When I experience this warning sign I have an urge to...

Action: When I experience this warning sign what I actually do is...

Reaction: I tend to invite others to become part of my problem by...

For reorders call: Herald House/Independence Press at 1-800-767-8181 or (816) 521-3015

Warning Sign Identification Card—Side 1

Title: _____

Description: I know I'm in trouble with my recovery when I...

Thought: When I experience this warning sign I tend to think...

Feeling: When I experience this warning sign I tend to feel...

Urge: When I experience this warning sign I have an urge to...

Action: When I experience this warning sign what I actually do is...

Reaction: I tend to invite others to become part of my problem by...

For reorders call: Herald House/Independence Press at 1-800-767-8181 or (816) 521-3015

Warning Sign Identification Card—Side 1

Title: _____

Description: I know I'm in trouble with my recovery when I...

Thought: When I experience this warning sign I tend to think...

Feeling: When I experience this warning sign I tend to feel...

Urge: When I experience this warning sign I have an urge to...

Action: When I experience this warning sign what I actually do is...

Reaction: I tend to invite others to become part of my problem by...

For reorders call: Herald House/Independence Press at 1-800-767-8181 or (816) 521-3015

Warning Sign Identification Card—Side 2

Title: _____

Recovery Activities: The recovery activities I can use to manage this warning sign are…

Managing Thoughts: A new way of thinking that will help me manage this warning sign is…

Managing Feelings: A new way of managing my feelings is…

Managing Urges: A new way of managing my urges is…

Managing Actions: A new way of acting is…

Managing Reactions: A new way of inviting people to help me is…

© 1995 Terence T. Gorski CENAPS®   Item #9780830913329

Warning Sign Identification Card—Side 2

Title: _____

Recovery Activities: The recovery activities I can use to manage this warning sign are…

Managing Thoughts: A new way of thinking that will help me manage this warning sign is…

Managing Feelings: A new way of managing my feelings is…

Managing Urges: A new way of managing my urges is…

Managing Actions: A new way of acting is…

Managing Reactions: A new way of inviting people to help me is…

© 1995 Terence T. Gorski CENAPS®   Item #9780830913329

Warning Sign Identification Card—Side 2

Title: _____

Recovery Activities: The recovery activities I can use to manage this warning sign are…

Managing Thoughts: A new way of thinking that will help me manage this warning sign is…

Managing Feelings: A new way of managing my feelings is…

Managing Urges: A new way of managing my urges is…

Managing Actions: A new way of acting is…

Managing Reactions: A new way of inviting people to help me is…

© 1995 Terence T. Gorski CENAPS®   Item #9780830913329

Warning Sign Identification Card—Side 2

Title: _____

Recovery Activities: The recovery activities I can use to manage this warning sign are…

Managing Thoughts: A new way of thinking that will help me manage this warning sign is…

Managing Feelings: A new way of managing my feelings is…

Managing Urges: A new way of managing my urges is…

Managing Actions: A new way of acting is…

Managing Reactions: A new way of inviting people to help me is…

© 1995 Terence T. Gorski CENAPS®   Item #9780830913329

Warning Sign Identification Card—Side 1

Title: _____

Description: I know I'm in trouble with my recovery when I...

Thought: When I experience this warning sign I tend to think...

Feeling: When I experience this warning sign I tend to feel...

Urge: When I experience this warning sign I have an urge to...

Action: When I experience this warning sign what I actually do is...

Reaction: I tend to invite others to become part of my problem by...

For reorders call: Herald House/Independence Press at 1-800-767-8181 or (816) 521-3015

Warning Sign Identification Card—Side 1

Title: _____

Description: I know I'm in trouble with my recovery when I...

Thought: When I experience this warning sign I tend to think...

Feeling: When I experience this warning sign I tend to feel...

Urge: When I experience this warning sign I have an urge to...

Action: When I experience this warning sign what I actually do is...

Reaction: I tend to invite others to become part of my problem by...

For reorders call: Herald House/Independence Press at 1-800-767-8181 or (816) 521-3015

Warning Sign Identification Card—Side 1

Title: _____

Description: I know I'm in trouble with my recovery when I...

Thought: When I experience this warning sign I tend to think...

Feeling: When I experience this warning sign I tend to feel...

Urge: When I experience this warning sign I have an urge to...

Action: When I experience this warning sign what I actually do is...

Reaction: I tend to invite others to become part of my problem by...

For reorders call: Herald House/Independence Press at 1-800-767-8181 or (816) 521-3015

Warning Sign Identification Card—Side 1

Title: _____

Description: I know I'm in trouble with my recovery when I...

Thought: When I experience this warning sign I tend to think...

Feeling: When I experience this warning sign I tend to feel...

Urge: When I experience this warning sign I have an urge to...

Action: When I experience this warning sign what I actually do is...

Reaction: I tend to invite others to become part of my problem by...

For reorders call: Herald House/Independence Press at 1-800-767-8181 or (816) 521-3015

Warning Sign Identification Card—Side 2

Title: _____

Recovery Activities: The recovery activities I can use to manage this warning sign are…

Managing Thoughts: A new way of thinking that will help me manage this warning sign is…

Managing Feelings: A new way of managing my feelings is…

Managing Urges: A new way of managing my urges is…

Managing Actions: A new way of acting is…

Managing Reactions: A new way of inviting people to help me is…

© 1995 Terence T. Gorski CENAPS®

Item #9780830913329

Warning Sign Identification Card—Side 2

Title: _____

Recovery Activities: The recovery activities I can use to manage this warning sign are…

Managing Thoughts: A new way of thinking that will help me manage this warning sign is…

Managing Feelings: A new way of managing my feelings is…

Managing Urges: A new way of managing my urges is…

Managing Actions: A new way of acting is…

Managing Reactions: A new way of inviting people to help me is…

© 1995 Terence T. Gorski CENAPS®

Item #9780830913329

Warning Sign Identification Card—Side 2

Title: _____

Recovery Activities: The recovery activities I can use to manage this warning sign are…

Managing Thoughts: A new way of thinking that will help me manage this warning sign is…

Managing Feelings: A new way of managing my feelings is…

Managing Urges: A new way of managing my urges is…

Managing Actions: A new way of acting is…

Managing Reactions: A new way of inviting people to help me is…

© 1995 Terence T. Gorski CENAPS®

Item #9780830913329

Warning Sign Identification Card—Side 2

Title: _____

Recovery Activities: The recovery activities I can use to manage this warning sign are…

Managing Thoughts: A new way of thinking that will help me manage this warning sign is…

Managing Feelings: A new way of managing my feelings is…

Managing Urges: A new way of managing my urges is…

Managing Actions: A new way of acting is…

Managing Reactions: A new way of inviting people to help me is…

© 1995 Terence T. Gorski CENAPS®

Item #9780830913329

Warning Sign Identification Card—Side 1

Title: _____

Description: I know I'm in trouble with my recovery when I...

_____
_____

Thought: When I experience this warning sign I tend to think...

_____
_____

Feeling: When I experience this warning sign I tend to feel...

_____
_____

Urge: When I experience this warning sign I have an urge to...

_____
_____

Action: When I experience this warning sign what I actually do is...

_____
_____

Reaction: I tend to invite others to become part of my problem by...

_____
_____

For reorders call: Herald House/Independence Press at 1-800-767-8181 or (816) 521-3015

Warning Sign Identification Card—Side 1

Title: _____

Description: I know I'm in trouble with my recovery when I...

_____
_____

Thought: When I experience this warning sign I tend to think...

_____
_____

Feeling: When I experience this warning sign I tend to feel...

_____
_____

Urge: When I experience this warning sign I have an urge to...

_____
_____

Action: When I experience this warning sign what I actually do is...

_____
_____

Reaction: I tend to invite others to become part of my problem by...

_____
_____

For reorders call: Herald House/Independence Press at 1-800-767-8181 or (816) 521-3015

Warning Sign Identification Card—Side 1

Title: _____

Description: I know I'm in trouble with my recovery when I...

_____
_____

Thought: When I experience this warning sign I tend to think...

_____
_____

Feeling: When I experience this warning sign I tend to feel...

_____
_____

Urge: When I experience this warning sign I have an urge to...

_____
_____

Action: When I experience this warning sign what I actually do is...

_____
_____

Reaction: I tend to invite others to become part of my problem by...

_____
_____

For reorders call: Herald House/Independence Press at 1-800-767-8181 or (816) 521-3015

Warning Sign Identification Card—Side 1

Title: _____

Description: I know I'm in trouble with my recovery when I...

_____
_____

Thought: When I experience this warning sign I tend to think...

_____
_____

Feeling: When I experience this warning sign I tend to feel...

_____
_____

Urge: When I experience this warning sign I have an urge to...

_____
_____

Action: When I experience this warning sign what I actually do is...

_____
_____

Reaction: I tend to invite others to become part of my problem by...

_____
_____

For reorders call: Herald House/Independence Press at 1-800-767-8181 or (816) 521-3015

Warning Sign Identification Card—Side 2

Title:

Recovery Activities: The recovery activities I can use to manage this warning sign are…

Managing Thoughts: A new way of thinking that will help me manage this warning sign is…

Managing Feelings: A new way of managing my feelings is…

Managing Urges: A new way of managing my urges is…

Managing Actions: A new way of acting is…

Managing Reactions: A new way of inviting people to help me is…

© 1995 Terence T. Gorski CENAPS®   Item #9780830913329

Warning Sign Identification Card—Side 2

Title:

Recovery Activities: The recovery activities I can use to manage this warning sign are…

Managing Thoughts: A new way of thinking that will help me manage this warning sign is…

Managing Feelings: A new way of managing my feelings is…

Managing Urges: A new way of managing my urges is…

Managing Actions: A new way of acting is…

Managing Reactions: A new way of inviting people to help me is…

© 1995 Terence T. Gorski CENAPS®   Item #9780830913329

Warning Sign Identification Card—Side 2

Title:

Recovery Activities: The recovery activities I can use to manage this warning sign are…

Managing Thoughts: A new way of thinking that will help me manage this warning sign is…

Managing Feelings: A new way of managing my feelings is…

Managing Urges: A new way of managing my urges is…

Managing Actions: A new way of acting is…

Managing Reactions: A new way of inviting people to help me is…

© 1995 Terence T. Gorski CENAPS®   Item #9780830913329

Warning Sign Identification Card—Side 2

Title:

Recovery Activities: The recovery activities I can use to manage this warning sign are…

Managing Thoughts: A new way of thinking that will help me manage this warning sign is…

Managing Feelings: A new way of managing my feelings is…

Managing Urges: A new way of managing my urges is…

Managing Actions: A new way of acting is…

Managing Reactions: A new way of inviting people to help me is…

© 1995 Terence T. Gorski CENAPS®   Item #9780830913329

Warning Sign Identification Card—Side 1

Title: _____

Description: I know I'm in trouble with my recovery when I...

Thought: When I experience this warning sign I tend to think...

Feeling: When I experience this warning sign I tend to feel...

Urge: When I experience this warning sign I have an urge to...

Action: When I experience this warning sign what I actually do is...

Reaction: I tend to invite others to become part of my problem by...

For reorders call: Herald House/Independence Press at 1-800-767-8181 or (816) 521-3015

Warning Sign Identification Card—Side 1

Title: _____

Description: I know I'm in trouble with my recovery when I...

Thought: When I experience this warning sign I tend to think...

Feeling: When I experience this warning sign I tend to feel...

Urge: When I experience this warning sign I have an urge to...

Action: When I experience this warning sign what I actually do is...

Reaction: I tend to invite others to become part of my problem by...

For reorders call: Herald House/Independence Press at 1-800-767-8181 or (816) 521-3015

Warning Sign Identification Card—Side 1

Title: _____

Description: I know I'm in trouble with my recovery when I...

Thought: When I experience this warning sign I tend to think...

Feeling: When I experience this warning sign I tend to feel...

Urge: When I experience this warning sign I have an urge to...

Action: When I experience this warning sign what I actually do is...

Reaction: I tend to invite others to become part of my problem by...

For reorders call: Herald House/Independence Press at 1-800-767-8181 or (816) 521-3015

Warning Sign Identification Card—Side 1

Title: _____

Description: I know I'm in trouble with my recovery when I...

Thought: When I experience this warning sign I tend to think...

Feeling: When I experience this warning sign I tend to feel...

Urge: When I experience this warning sign I have an urge to...

Action: When I experience this warning sign what I actually do is...

Reaction: I tend to invite others to become part of my problem by...

For reorders call: Herald House/Independence Press at 1-800-767-8181 or (816) 521-3015

Warning Sign Identification Card—Side 2

Title: _____

Recovery Activities: The recovery activities I can use to manage this warning sign are…

Managing Thoughts: A new way of thinking that will help me manage this warning sign is…

Managing Feelings: A new way of managing my feelings is…

Managing Urges: A new way of managing my urges is…

Managing Actions: A new way of acting is…

Managing Reactions: A new way of inviting people to help me is…

Item #9780830913329

Warning Sign Identification Card—Side 2

Title: _____

Recovery Activities: The recovery activities I can use to manage this warning sign are…

Managing Thoughts: A new way of thinking that will help me manage this warning sign is…

Managing Feelings: A new way of managing my feelings is…

Managing Urges: A new way of managing my urges is…

Managing Actions: A new way of acting is…

Managing Reactions: A new way of inviting people to help me is…

Item #9780830913329

Warning Sign Identification Card—Side 2

Title: _____

Recovery Activities: The recovery activities I can use to manage this warning sign are…

Managing Thoughts: A new way of thinking that will help me manage this warning sign is…

Managing Feelings: A new way of managing my feelings is…

Managing Urges: A new way of managing my urges is…

Managing Actions: A new way of acting is…

Managing Reactions: A new way of inviting people to help me is…

© 1995 Terence T. Gorski CENAPS®

Item #9780830913329

Warning Sign Identification Card—Side 2

Title: _____

Recovery Activities: The recovery activities I can use to manage this warning sign are…

Managing Thoughts: A new way of thinking that will help me manage this warning sign is…

Managing Feelings: A new way of managing my feelings is…

Managing Urges: A new way of managing my urges is…

Managing Actions: A new way of acting is…

Managing Reactions: A new way of inviting people to help me is…

© 1995 Terence T. Gorski CENAPS®

Item #9780830913329

Warning Sign Identification Card—Side 1

Title: _____

Description: I know I'm in trouble with my recovery when I...
_____

Thought: When I experience this warning sign I tend to think...
_____

Feeling: When I experience this warning sign I tend to feel...
_____

Urge: When I experience this warning sign I have an urge to...
_____

Action: When I experience this warning sign what I actually do is...
_____

Reaction: I tend to invite others to become part of my problem by...
_____

For reorders call: Herald House/Independence Press at 1-800-767-8181 or (816) 521-3015

Warning Sign Identification Card—Side 1

Title: _____

Description: I know I'm in trouble with my recovery when I...
_____

Thought: When I experience this warning sign I tend to think...
_____

Feeling: When I experience this warning sign I tend to feel...
_____

Urge: When I experience this warning sign I have an urge to...
_____

Action: When I experience this warning sign what I actually do is...
_____

Reaction: I tend to invite others to become part of my problem by...
_____

For reorders call: Herald House/Independence Press at 1-800-767-8181 or (816) 521-3015

Warning Sign Identification Card—Side 1

Title: _____

Description: I know I'm in trouble with my recovery when I...
_____

Thought: When I experience this warning sign I tend to think...
_____

Feeling: When I experience this warning sign I tend to feel...
_____

Urge: When I experience this warning sign I have an urge to...
_____

Action: When I experience this warning sign what I actually do is...
_____

Reaction: I tend to invite others to become part of my problem by...
_____

For reorders call: Herald House/Independence Press at 1-800-767-8181 or (816) 521-3015

Warning Sign Identification Card—Side 1

Title: _____

Description: I know I'm in trouble with my recovery when I...
_____

Thought: When I experience this warning sign I tend to think...
_____

Feeling: When I experience this warning sign I tend to feel...
_____

Urge: When I experience this warning sign I have an urge to...
_____

Action: When I experience this warning sign what I actually do is...
_____

Reaction: I tend to invite others to become part of my problem by...
_____

For reorders call: Herald House/Independence Press at 1-800-767-8181 or (816) 521-3015

Warning Sign Identification Card—Side 2

Title: _____

Recovery Activities: The recovery activities I can use to manage this warning sign are…

Managing Thoughts: A new way of thinking that will help me manage this warning sign is…

Managing Feelings: A new way of managing my feelings is…

Managing Urges: A new way of managing my urges is…

Managing Actions: A new way of acting is…

Managing Reactions: A new way of inviting people to help me is…

© 1995 Terence T. Gorski CENAPS®

Item #9780830913329

Warning Sign Identification Card—Side 2

Title: _____

Recovery Activities: The recovery activities I can use to manage this warning sign are…

Managing Thoughts: A new way of thinking that will help me manage this warning sign is…

Managing Feelings: A new way of managing my feelings is…

Managing Urges: A new way of managing my urges is…

Managing Actions: A new way of acting is…

Managing Reactions: A new way of inviting people to help me is…

© 1995 Terence T. Gorski CENAPS®

Item #9780830913329

Warning Sign Identification Card—Side 2

Title: _____

Recovery Activities: The recovery activities I can use to manage this warning sign are…

Managing Thoughts: A new way of thinking that will help me manage this warning sign is…

Managing Feelings: A new way of managing my feelings is…

Managing Urges: A new way of managing my urges is…

Managing Actions: A new way of acting is…

Managing Reactions: A new way of inviting people to help me is…

© 1995 Terence T. Gorski CENAPS®

Item #9780830913329

Warning Sign Identification Card—Side 2

Title: _____

Recovery Activities: The recovery activities I can use to manage this warning sign are…

Managing Thoughts: A new way of thinking that will help me manage this warning sign is…

Managing Feelings: A new way of managing my feelings is…

Managing Urges: A new way of managing my urges is…

Managing Actions: A new way of acting is…

Managing Reactions: A new way of inviting people to help me is…

© 1995 Terence T. Gorski CENAPS®

Item #9780830913329

Warning Sign Identification Card—Side 1

Title: _____

Description: I know I'm in trouble with my recovery when I…

_____

_____

Thought: When I experience this warning sign I tend to think…

_____

_____

Feeling: When I experience this warning sign I tend to feel…

_____

_____

Urge: When I experience this warning sign I have an urge to…

_____

_____

Action: When I experience this warning sign what I actually do is…

_____

_____

Reaction: I tend to invite others to become part of my problem by…

_____

_____

For reorders call: Herald House/Independence Press at 1-800-767-8181 or (816) 521-3015

Warning Sign Identification Card—Side 1

Title: _____

Description: I know I'm in trouble with my recovery when I…

_____

_____

Thought: When I experience this warning sign I tend to think…

_____

_____

Feeling: When I experience this warning sign I tend to feel…

_____

_____

Urge: When I experience this warning sign I have an urge to…

_____

_____

Action: When I experience this warning sign what I actually do is…

_____

_____

Reaction: I tend to invite others to become part of my problem by…

_____

_____

For reorders call: Herald House/Independence Press at 1-800-767-8181 or (816) 521-3015

Warning Sign Identification Card—Side 1

Title: _____

Description: I know I'm in trouble with my recovery when I…

_____

_____

Thought: When I experience this warning sign I tend to think…

_____

_____

Feeling: When I experience this warning sign I tend to feel…

_____

_____

Urge: When I experience this warning sign I have an urge to…

_____

_____

Action: When I experience this warning sign what I actually do is…

_____

_____

Reaction: I tend to invite others to become part of my problem by…

_____

_____

For reorders call: Herald House/Independence Press at 1-800-767-8181 or (816) 521-3015

Warning Sign Identification Card—Side 1

Title: _____

Description: I know I'm in trouble with my recovery when I…

_____

_____

Thought: When I experience this warning sign I tend to think…

_____

_____

Feeling: When I experience this warning sign I tend to feel…

_____

_____

Urge: When I experience this warning sign I have an urge to…

_____

_____

Action: When I experience this warning sign what I actually do is…

_____

_____

Reaction: I tend to invite others to become part of my problem by…

_____

_____

For reorders call: Herald House/Independence Press at 1-800-767-8181 or (816) 521-3015

Warning Sign Identification Card—Side 2

Title:___

Recovery Activities: The recovery activities I can use to manage this warning sign are…

Managing Thoughts: A new way of thinking that will help me manage this warning sign is…

Managing Feelings: A new way of managing my feelings is…

Managing Urges: A new way of managing my urges is…

Managing Actions: A new way of acting is…

Managing Reactions: A new way of inviting people to help me is…

© 1995 Terence T. Gorski CENAPS®

Item #9780830913329

Warning Sign Identification Card—Side 2

Title:___

Recovery Activities: The recovery activities I can use to manage this warning sign are…

Managing Thoughts: A new way of thinking that will help me manage this warning sign is…

Managing Feelings: A new way of managing my feelings is…

Managing Urges: A new way of managing my urges is…

Managing Actions: A new way of acting is…

Managing Reactions: A new way of inviting people to help me is…

© 1995 Terence T. Gorski CENAPS®

Item #9780830913329

Warning Sign Identification Card—Side 2

Title:___

Recovery Activities: The recovery activities I can use to manage this warning sign are…

Managing Thoughts: A new way of thinking that will help me manage this warning sign is…

Managing Feelings: A new way of managing my feelings is…

Managing Urges: A new way of managing my urges is…

Managing Actions: A new way of acting is…

Managing Reactions: A new way of inviting people to help me is…

© 1995 Terence T. Gorski CENAPS®

Item #9780830913329

Warning Sign Identification Card—Side 2

Title:___

Recovery Activities: The recovery activities I can use to manage this warning sign are…

Managing Thoughts: A new way of thinking that will help me manage this warning sign is…

Managing Feelings: A new way of managing my feelings is…

Managing Urges: A new way of managing my urges is…

Managing Actions: A new way of acting is…

Managing Reactions: A new way of inviting people to help me is…

© 1995 Terence T. Gorski CENAPS®

Item #9780830913329

Warning Sign Identification Card—Side 1

Title: _____

Description: I know I'm in trouble with my recovery when I...

Thought: When I experience this warning sign I tend to think...

Feeling: When I experience this warning sign I tend to feel...

Urge: When I experience this warning sign I have an urge to...

Action: When I experience this warning sign what I actually do is...

Reaction: I tend to invite others to become part of my problem by...

For reorders call: Herald House/Independence Press at 1-800-767-8181 or (816) 521-3015

Warning Sign Identification Card—Side 1

Title: _____

Description: I know I'm in trouble with my recovery when I...

Thought: When I experience this warning sign I tend to think...

Feeling: When I experience this warning sign I tend to feel...

Urge: When I experience this warning sign I have an urge to...

Action: When I experience this warning sign what I actually do is...

Reaction: I tend to invite others to become part of my problem by...

For reorders call: Herald House/Independence Press at 1-800-767-8181 or (816) 521-3015

Warning Sign Identification Card—Side 1

Title: _____

Description: I know I'm in trouble with my recovery when I...

Thought: When I experience this warning sign I tend to think...

Feeling: When I experience this warning sign I tend to feel...

Urge: When I experience this warning sign I have an urge to...

Action: When I experience this warning sign what I actually do is...

Reaction: I tend to invite others to become part of my problem by...

For reorders call: Herald House/Independence Press at 1-800-767-8181 or (816) 521-3015

Warning Sign Identification Card—Side 1

Title: _____

Description: I know I'm in trouble with my recovery when I...

Thought: When I experience this warning sign I tend to think...

Feeling: When I experience this warning sign I tend to feel...

Urge: When I experience this warning sign I have an urge to...

Action: When I experience this warning sign what I actually do is...

Reaction: I tend to invite others to become part of my problem by...

For reorders call: Herald House/Independence Press at 1-800-767-8181 or (816) 521-3015

Warning Sign Identification Card—Side 2

Title: _____

Recovery Activities: The recovery activities I can use to manage this warning sign are…

Managing Thoughts: A new way of thinking that will help me manage this warning sign is…

Managing Feelings: A new way of managing my feelings is…

Managing Urges: A new way of managing my urges is…

Managing Actions: A new way of acting is…

Managing Reactions: A new way of inviting people to help me is…

© 1995 Terence T. Gorski CENAPS®

Item #9780830913329

Warning Sign Identification Card—Side 2

Item #9780830913329

© 1995 Terence T. Gorski CENAPS®

Managing Reactions: A new way of inviting people to help me is…

Managing Actions: A new way of acting is…

Managing Urges: A new way of managing my urges is…

Managing Feelings: A new way of managing my feelings is…

Managing Thoughts: A new way of thinking that will help me manage this warning sign is…

Title: _____

Recovery Activities: The recovery activities I can use to manage this warning sign are…

© 1995 Terence T. Gorski CENAPS®

Warning Sign Identification Card—Side 2

Title: _____

Recovery Activities: The recovery activities I can use to manage this warning sign are…

Managing Thoughts: A new way of thinking that will help me manage this warning sign is…

Managing Feelings: A new way of managing my feelings is…

Managing Urges: A new way of managing my urges is…

Managing Actions: A new way of acting is…

Managing Reactions: A new way of inviting people to help me is…

© 1995 Terence T. Gorski CENAPS®

Item #9780830913329

Warning Sign Identification Card—Side 1

Title: _____

Description: I know I'm in trouble with my recovery when I...

Thought: When I experience this warning sign I tend to think...

Feeling: When I experience this warning sign I tend to feel...

Urge: When I experience this warning sign I have an urge to...

Action: When I experience this warning sign what I actually do is...

Reaction: I tend to invite others to become part of my problem by...

For reorders call: Herald House/Independence Press at 1-800-767-8181 or (816) 521-3015

Warning Sign Identification Card—Side 1

Title: _____

Description: I know I'm in trouble with my recovery when I...

Thought: When I experience this warning sign I tend to think...

Feeling: When I experience this warning sign I tend to feel...

Urge: When I experience this warning sign I have an urge to...

Action: When I experience this warning sign what I actually do is...

Reaction: I tend to invite others to become part of my problem by...

For reorders call: Herald House/Independence Press at 1-800-767-8181 or (816) 521-3015

Warning Sign Identification Card—Side 1

Title: _____

Description: I know I'm in trouble with my recovery when I...

Thought: When I experience this warning sign I tend to think...

Feeling: When I experience this warning sign I tend to feel...

Urge: When I experience this warning sign I have an urge to...

Action: When I experience this warning sign what I actually do is...

Reaction: I tend to invite others to become part of my problem by...

For reorders call: Herald House/Independence Press at 1-800-767-8181 or (816) 521-3015

Warning Sign Identification Card—Side 1

Title: _____

Description: I know I'm in trouble with my recovery when I...

Thought: When I experience this warning sign I tend to think...

Feeling: When I experience this warning sign I tend to feel...

Urge: When I experience this warning sign I have an urge to...

Action: When I experience this warning sign what I actually do is...

Reaction: I tend to invite others to become part of my problem by...

For reorders call: Herald House/Independence Press at 1-800-767-8181 or (816) 521-3015

Warning Sign Identification Card—Side 2

Title: _____

Recovery Activities: The recovery activities I can use to manage this warning sign are…

Managing Thoughts: A new way of thinking that will help me manage this warning sign is…

Managing Feelings: A new way of managing my feelings is…

Managing Urges: A new way of managing my urges is…

Managing Actions: A new way of acting is…

Managing Reactions: A new way of inviting people to help me is…

© 1995 Terence T. Gorski CENAPS®   Item #9780830913329

Warning Sign Identification Card—Side 2

Title: _____

Recovery Activities: The recovery activities I can use to manage this warning sign are…

Managing Thoughts: A new way of thinking that will help me manage this warning sign is…

Managing Feelings: A new way of managing my feelings is…

Managing Urges: A new way of managing my urges is…

Managing Actions: A new way of acting is…

Managing Reactions: A new way of inviting people to help me is…

© 1995 Terence T. Gorski CENAPS®   Item #9780830913329

Warning Sign Identification Card—Side 2

Title: _____

Recovery Activities: The recovery activities I can use to manage this warning sign are…

Managing Thoughts: A new way of thinking that will help me manage this warning sign is…

Managing Feelings: A new way of managing my feelings is…

Managing Urges: A new way of managing my urges is…

Managing Actions: A new way of acting is…

Managing Reactions: A new way of inviting people to help me is…

© 1995 Terence T. Gorski CENAPS®   Item #9780830913329

Warning Sign Identification Card—Side 2

Title: _____

Recovery Activities: The recovery activities I can use to manage this warning sign are…

Managing Thoughts: A new way of thinking that will help me manage this warning sign is…

Managing Feelings: A new way of managing my feelings is…

Managing Urges: A new way of managing my urges is…

Managing Actions: A new way of acting is…

Managing Reactions: A new way of inviting people to help me is…

© 1995 Terence T. Gorski CENAPS®   Item #9780830913329

Warning Sign Identification Card—Side 1

Title: _____

Description: I know I'm in trouble with my recovery when I...

_____

Thought: When I experience this warning sign I tend to think...

_____

Feeling: When I experience this warning sign I tend to feel...

_____

Urge: When I experience this warning sign I have an urge to...

_____

Action: When I experience this warning sign what I actually do is...

_____

Reaction: I tend to invite others to become part of my problem by...

_____

For reorders call: Herald House/Independence Press at 1-800-767-8181 or (816) 521-3015

Warning Sign Identification Card—Side 1

Title: _____

Description: I know I'm in trouble with my recovery when I...

_____

Thought: When I experience this warning sign I tend to think...

_____

Feeling: When I experience this warning sign I tend to feel...

_____

Urge: When I experience this warning sign I have an urge to...

_____

Action: When I experience this warning sign what I actually do is...

_____

Reaction: I tend to invite others to become part of my problem by...

_____

For reorders call: Herald House/Independence Press at 1-800-767-8181 or (816) 521-3015

Warning Sign Identification Card—Side 1

Title: _____

Description: I know I'm in trouble with my recovery when I...

_____

Thought: When I experience this warning sign I tend to think...

_____

Feeling: When I experience this warning sign I tend to feel...

_____

Urge: When I experience this warning sign I have an urge to...

_____

Action: When I experience this warning sign what I actually do is...

_____

Reaction: I tend to invite others to become part of my problem by...

_____

For reorders call: Herald House/Independence Press at 1-800-767-8181 or (816) 521-3015

THE CENAPS® CORPORATION
TRAINING • CONSULTATION • RESEARCH

Please send me information on the Relapse Prevention Certification School.

Name _____

Title _____

Organization _____

Work Address _____

Work City/State/Zip _____

Home Address _____

Home City/State/Zip _____

Work Phone _____

Home Phone _____

Warning Sign Identification Card—Side 2

Title: _____

Recovery Activities: The recovery activities I can use to manage this warning sign are…

_____

Managing Thoughts: A new way of thinking that will help me manage this warning sign is…

_____

Managing Feelings: A new way of managing my feelings is…

_____

Managing Urges: A new way of managing my urges is…

_____

Managing Actions: A new way of acting is…

_____

Managing Reactions: A new way of inviting people to help me is…

_____

© 1995 Terence T. Gorski CENAPS®   Item #9780830913329

Warning Sign Identification Card—Side 2

Title: _____

Recovery Activities: The recovery activities I can use to manage this warning sign are…

_____

Managing Thoughts: A new way of thinking that will help me manage this warning sign is…

_____

Managing Feelings: A new way of managing my feelings is…

_____

Managing Urges: A new way of managing my urges is…

_____

Managing Actions: A new way of acting is…

_____

Managing Reactions: A new way of inviting people to help me is…

_____

© 1995 Terence T. Gorski CENAPS®   Item #9780830913329

Warning Sign Identification Card—Side 2

Title: _____

Recovery Activities: The recovery activities I can use to manage this warning sign are…

_____

Managing Thoughts: A new way of thinking that will help me manage this warning sign is…

_____

Managing Feelings: A new way of managing my feelings is…

_____

Managing Urges: A new way of managing my urges is…

_____

Managing Actions: A new way of acting is…

_____

Managing Reactions: A new way of inviting people to help me is…

_____

© 1995 Terence T. Gorski CENAPS®   Item #9780830913329

The Center for Applied Sciences
The CENAPS® Corporation
13194 Spring Hill Drive
Spring Hill, FL 34609